That's a crock, Barack

By Fred J. Eckert

President Obama's record of saying
things that are untrue, duplicitous,
arrogant and delusional.
or
Barack Obama's lies.
and
Why Obama should not be re-elected.

Beestone Books
P.O. Box 97785
Raleigh, North Carolina 27624-7785
BeestoneBooks@gmail.com

Cover illustration and design by Ted Williams
(whcom@frontiernet.net)

ISBN 978-0-9850055-0-4

TO:
My wife, Karen
and our children– Doug, Brian and Cindy

and our grandchildren–
Mary Olivia, Luke, Sophie and Pete

Introduction

This was the moment when we should have spotted the crock and con.

"I am absolutely certain that generations from now, we will be able to look back and tell our children that this was the moment when we began to provide care for the sick and good jobs to the jobless; this was the moment when the rise of the oceans began to slow and our planet began to heal."

Barack Hussein Obama
3 June 2008

Try to think of anything that any other presidential nominee ever said that comes even remotely close to the vainglorious prognostication that Barack Obama read to us from his teleprompter that evening as he celebrated and savored his becoming the presumptive Democratic nominee for president.

Barack was "absolutely certain" about what he was claiming here?

What an astonishing statement.

What a crock!

That he would make such a claim should have given the American people such great pause as to rule out any possibility that he could be elected President of the United States.

That it did not– and that neither did the many other outrageous things he said during his quest for the presidency— is compelling confirmation that his political campaign team and their cheerleading squad in the mainstream media are extraordinarily effective con artists.

The public fell for their pitch proclaiming Barack to be so deep and so bright, brilliant even— a gallant leader speaking majestic thoughts, some magical, near-messianic figure the likes of which Americans had never before been so blessed to have appear amongst us to show us the errors of our ways and to shape us into a better people as he proceeds to remake the world in his own image.

It was such a great con. Such an utter crock.

He was for hope!

He was for change!

Oh wow! Oh wow! Oh wow!

But it was all truly no more than sly, scheming shrewd theatre.

The suggestion that the Obama campaign and the media jointly propagandized with such amazing success–

a spectacular deception given how their challenge was to depict this tiny pond as a vast ocean— was that the things that Barack said were profound; that he was an inspired and inspiring leader with a grand vision that the nation needed to grasp and act upon.

Their proof?

Look, see, the audiences are so large!

Look, see, some people are cheering so loudly!

Now and then someone fainted, or pretended to, while listening to Barack speak, and the spin from the Obama campaign and its news media collaborators was: more proof!

And don't forget the settings! Still more proof.

He spoke in Berlin— just like Reagan and Kennedy had when they were president. But Barack did it even before he got elected president!

So, see, he must belong right up there with Reagan and Kennedy.

Want proof that he'd be great at foreign affairs? Just watch how he can make trips overseas! Look, see, there he is giving a campaign speech before a *foreign* audience!

He even had his very own very official-looking make-believe seal often placed on the front of the podiums behind which he stood. He has a seal! Just like someone who *is* president!

When he delivered his nomination acceptance speech he did so on a stage configured like a Greek or Roman temple, emerging from between gigantic columns, just like some great emperor might have done! And it was outdoors, just like John F. Kennedy's acceptance speech had been! But Barack's was on the 50-yard-line of an NFL football stadium! Like a rock concert extravaganza at the Super Bowl! And there was a fantastic fireworks display, too!

It was all about how and where Barack said the things he said.

Never, or very rarely ever, about the substance.

But what about the things he actually says?

Barack Hussein Obama, it turns out, has a pattern of saying things that are untrue, delusional, arrogant, self-indulgent, absurd, silly, ludicrous, laughable and just plain wrong.

This book features a representative sampling.

Again: just try to think of anything that any other presidential nominee ever said that comes even remotely close to the vainglorious absurdity of what Barack read to us from his teleprompter that evening of June 3, 2008.

Read the words again and then really think about the thought that Barack expressed that evening. Reflect upon how he assessed this turn of events and how he believed that we and future generations ought to— and would— treasure it:

"I am absolutely certain that generations from now, we will be able to look back and tell our children that this was the moment when we began to provide care for the sick and good jobs to the jobless; this was the moment when the rise of the oceans began to slow and our planet began to heal.

Who but a delusional megalomaniac could profess to believe what Obama was claiming?

"The moment" to which Barack Obama was referring was nothing more than the declaration by the news media that he had accumulated enough delegates to secure his party's nomination.

That's it! Really. Seriously. No joke.

Barack was "absolutely certain" it marked a turning point in American and world history so stupendous— right up there with other unparalleled moments of the ages – that future generations would marvel about it to their children – "absolutely certain."

Not until he secured the nomination had we begun to provide care for the sick?

What were we doing with the sick before this moment arrived on June 3, 2008?

We had not begun to have doctors, nurses, medicines or hospitals— you know, people and things that provide for the sick— until this moment that the nomination fell to him?

Should we be looking back to that day and telling our children that all these good jobs that the formerly jobless now have can be traced to that moment that the Democrats picked Barack Obama over Hillary Clinton?

(But aren't there far more jobless now?)

If we check out the oceans today will we notice that they're not rising as fast as they were before he went over the top in the delegate count?

Barack could and would slow the rise of the oceans for us?

Just like God did for Noah?

Can we see and sense how the planet is healing?

Wouldn't be healing like it's doing right now had he not edged out Hillary Clinton for the nomination rather than the other way around, would it?

Could a candidate for President of the United States or a President of the United States really think and say things that are so mind-bogglingly absurd and arrogant?

Yes, he can! Yes, he can!

It's what Barack does.

Amazingly, he does it all the time.

It's time to call him on it.

It's time that the American people realize that we have been royally conned.

It's time for us to decide that we have had enough of narcissism, duplicity and ineptitude in the White House.

We need to resolve that come Election Day we shall stand up and respond as we should have four years ago: "That's a crock, Barack."

Fred J. Eckert

How great Thou art,
how great Thou art!

Singing the praises of Barack
(Performed by Barack)

Insights into why he thinks he is at least
our 4th greatest president
—even possibly the greatest.

"I would put our legislative and foreign policy accomplishments in our first two years against any president with the possible exceptions of Johnson, FDR and Lincoln— just in terms of what we've gotten done in modern history."

Did Barack really claim during his December 11, 2011, interview on CBS's *60 Minutes* that he may be the greatest president that the United States of America has ever had?

Yes, he did.

Can he be delusional enough to think such a thing and foolish enough to say it?

Yes, he can! Yes, he can!

To be fair, he did not claim that he is the greatest, just that he may be.

He clearly stated that it was "possible" that he is only the fourth greatest.

Lyndon Johnson, Franklin Roosevelt and Abraham Lincoln *might* have been even greater. He admits to this *possibility*.

So he may rank first, may rank second, may rank third.

But— no question about it— he ranks at least in the top four.

He rules out the possibility that three of the four American presidents who grace Mount Rushmore— George Washington, Thomas Jefferson and Theodore Roosevelt – might possibly match him.

Ronald Reagan? John Kennedy? Dwight Eisenhower? Andrew Jackson? James Monroe? James Madison? In Obama's mind— and he's not shy about saying so— not one of them is in the same league with him.

Nor, apparently, is the one president whom most Americans do seem to view as deserving to be in the same league with Obama, even perhaps a cut above— Jimmy Carter.

Question:

If Barack uttered a boast this outrageous, how come so few of us are aware of it?

ॐ

Answer: See opposite page.

Wondering why you can't seem to remember all the news media coverage about Barack's "I'm the greatest" braggadocio during that December 11, 2011, *60 Minutes* interview with Steve Kroft?

Because while Barack may not have the good sense to realize that making such a laughable claim might subject him to great ridicule and help American voters understand what a narcissist he really is, Steve Kroft and the other stanch Obama boosters at CBS do.

So CBS covered for Obama. They edited the tape to keep the *60 Minutes* audience from viewing the bit in the interview in which Barack spouted this ludicrous nonsense. But they made the mistake of publishing a transcript of the interview in its entirety.

That a supposedly professional journalist would not question, let alone challenge, such an absurd claim and that any news organization, especially a major one, would endeavor to cover up rather than play up such a far-fetched boast by a President of the United States, speaks volumes.

If you don't think this is a blatant case of media bias in support of Barack, consider the sort of Obama-boosting media bias propaganda that CBS left in:

KROFT: *You definitely have some impressive accomplishments.*

PRESIDENT OBAMA: *Thank you, Steve.*

KROFT: *No, you do. And more than a lot of presidents who manage to get reelected. My question is, is it enough? Why do you think you deserve to be reelected?*

CBS did not bill the Obama campaign for airing in prime time an hour long campaign commercial masquerading as a news interview.

Nor did they charge for the cover up job.

"I think that I'm a better speechwriter than my speechwriters. I know more about policies on any particular issue than my policy directors. And I'll tell you right now that I'm gonna think I'm a better political director than my political director."

Yes, he really said that— in an interview published in *New Yorker* magazine.

He's the greatest!

Just ask.

Actually, when the subject is how great he is, Barack's policy is: Don't even have to ask, I'll tell.

Of course it did not occur to *New Yorker* magazine, just as it so seldom does to others in the mainstream media, to ask Barack the sort of questions they would never hesitate to ask of any candidate or office holder who is a conservative.

Does he really believe that he cannot find anyone— *anyone*— who can write as well as he can?

If he is such a great speech writer, why doesn't he write his own speeches?

He knows more about every public policy issue than *anyone* else?

Every single one of them?

He's an expert on *everything*?

If he is admitting that the persons to whom he turns for advice on any given issue know less about it than he does, doesn't that raise this question: Why hire any advisors?

"Just give me the ball."

శ

"I'm LeBron, baby. I can play on this level. I got some game."

He's even greater than Michael Jordan?

"Just give me the ball" is what Barack said in reply to an email he received from his campaign director Patrick Gaspard following his first debate against John McCain in which Gaspard gushed: "You are more clutch than Michael Jordan."

And Michael Jordan isn't the only basketball legend who makes Barack think of Barack.

Back in 2004 when author David Mendell asked him how he saw his potential as national political figure, that time Barack compared himself to LeBron James.

Probably just a coincidence that LeBron's nickname is "King James."

To be fair, he did end up playing on the national level.

Playing – as opposed to *working*.

And, let's be fair, there is some slight similarity between Barack and Michael Jordan and between Barack and LeBron James:

Michael and LeBron each excel at putting a ball into a hole and Barack has put the country into a hole.

"Well, the big difference here and in '94
was you've got me."

જી

Bill Clinton famously said that "it depends on what the definition of 'is' is" and got some unintended laughs for sounding so Jesuitical— but his English language usage was correct.

Barack, it appears, does not know when to use "was" and when to use "is."

Poor as his English was, that's not what bothered the people who were listening to Obama's "no worries" pitch this day in January 2010.

The nervous Democratic members of Congress who had asked to meet with him could see the handwriting on the wall: it was looking like the mid-term elections might be as bad, perhaps even worse, for them than the 1994 mid-terms that had ushered out 40 years of Democratic Party dominance of the House of Representatives.

No worries, all is well, Barack assured them. This time they had going for them the "big difference" of *him*.

In 1994, the Republicans picked up 54 seats in the House to take control.

In 2010 they did so by picking up 63 seats, the largest seat change since 1948 and the largest for any midterm election since 1938.

It was indeed a "big difference."

And, yes, they have Barack to thank for it.

"She had fought a tough battle for four years. All through the campaign she was fighting, but finally she succumbed. And she insisted she's gonna be buried in an Obama t-shirt."

೮೦

Those Democratic congressmen in attendance at that January 2010 meeting may not have been grateful that what they had going for them was Barack, but in a speech he delivered in February 2010 Barack reminded them and the rest of us just how grateful we should be for his presence.

He told us the tale of the grateful dead woman.

In a speech touting newly enacted ObamaCare he included, as was his pattern, a sob story, the point of this one being to suggest that the reason some woman who campaigned for him had died after a prolonged bout with cancer was because she had lacked the sort of health care coverage she would have had had she not become ill before he became president.

A number of those Democratic congressmen may end up buried in a conservative Republican landslide at the polls, but, look folks, notice that I am so appreciated and venerated that some woman chose to be buried in a t-shirt that proclaims how great I am.

Can you think of any President of the United States other than Barack Obama who would make such a boast?

Narcissistic nuttiness?

Is it ever.

"I've written two books. I actually wrote them myself!"

౪

When Barack appeared before a gathering of teachers during the 2008 campaign and bragged that he had authored two books – "actually wrote them myself!"— the audience burst into laughter.

They laughed *with* Barack about his insinuation that those other politicians didn't possess the smarts to write books all by themselves like he did.

But a strong case can be made that they should have laughed *at* rather than *with* Barack.

Besides its being laughable for someone whose greatest experiences and achievements in life were being a "community organizer" and a state senator and spending mere months in the US Senate to have written two books about *himself*, there is also serious doubt as to the truthfulness of Barack's claim that Barack is the person who wrote Barack's books.

In his book *Deconstructing Obama*, author Jack Cashill makes a highly persuasive case that Obama's *Dreams From My Father* was really written by Obama friend and political mentor William Ayers, the unrepentant terrorist co-founder of the communist Weather Underground. He points out spelling errors in Barack's book identical to those in a book by Ayers. Cashill also makes a highly persuasive case that Obama's *The Audacity of Hope* was also written by someone other than Barack.

In his pro-Obama book *Barack and Michelle: Portrait of An American Marriage*, Christopher Andersen reports Michelle urged Barack to seek Ayers' help, that Barack delivered "a truckload" of tapes, notes and papers to Ayers and concludes: "In the end, Ayers' contribution to Barack's *Dreams From My Father* would be significant— so much so that the book's language, oddly specific references, literary devices, and themes would bear a jarring similarity to Ayers' own writing."

"You know I listen to, sometimes, these reporters on the news, 'Well, why haven't you solved world hunger yet? Why? It's been nine months!'"

෮

What's with the whining?

While it is certainly true that just about every office holder or candidate, not just Barack, is now and then annoyed by some in the media asking a difficult question or setting up an exaggerated expectation that is simply unrealistic, Barack Obama should be the last one to whine that the media is unfair to him.

The media has been aggressively indifferent when it comes to holding Barack to the same standard it holds other public figures, passing again and again on putting obvious questions to him when his being asked might present a problem for him, regularly going over the top in extolling exuberant praise upon him and even often covering up for him.

To Barack, it appears, any lull in the non-stop adulation is unfair criticism.

*"I will listen to you, especially
when we disagree."*

&

Barack's all ears!

So he proclaimed among the remarks he made the night of his election to the presidency.

Nice words.

Actions, of course, speak louder.

Truth is, Barack's a poor listener – especially when it comes to hearing things with which he disagrees.

The big test to find out whether he meant what he said was the discussion surrounding his wanting to overhaul health care.

"I won," he barked during a discussion with members of Congress who disagreed with what he was determined to ram through rather than hear them out.

When he suggested that some so-called super committee could point the way to getting the country's fiscal mess in order, he never bothered to work with it and when it failed was quick to claim that it was because others didn't listen.

"There are still too many Republicans in Congress who refuse to listen to the voices of reason and compromise that are coming from outside of Washington," he said.

With Barack, saying you'll listen really means never having to listen because you can always blame the other side for not listening.

"But I don't want the folks who created the mess to do a lot of talking. I want them to get out of the way so we can clean up the mess. I don't mind cleaning up after them, but don't do a lot of talking."

ଙ୍ଖ

Wait a moment. Wasn't Barack the guy who promised that as president he would listen, especially when he disagreed?

Well, why did he then later say that he doesn't want the folks who created the mess to do a lot of talking?

If they aren't talking, how can he listen to them?

Presumably he disagrees with "the folks who created the mess."

So...shouldn't he *especially* want to listen to them?

Why would you order people whom you especially want to listen to, "Don't do a lot of talking"?

*"The fundamental belief that **I am my brother's keeper**, I am my sister's keeper, that's the promise we need to keep. That's the change we need right now."*

෨

At the very time Barack Obama was spouting this "I am my brother's keeper" boast and admonition during his speech accepting the Democratic Party nomination for President of the United States in 2008, his brother George Hussein Onyango Obama was living in a filthy slum on the outskirts of Nairobi, Kenya, in a 6 foot by 9 foot makeshift shack without electricity, a toilet or even running water.

"I live here on less than a dollar a month," the Italian edition of *Vanity Fair* had earlier quoted him. A number of major European outlets reported this. The U.S. media either played it down or covered it up.

Although Barack was rich – his 2008 income exceeded $4 million – he never assisted his pitifully poor brother.

He kept right on raking in plenty of money, signed another lucrative book contract days before taking office as President and— secure in the knowledge that he is certain to become far richer in the years to come— continued to ignore the pathetic plight of his own younger brother.

For poor George Hussein Onyango Obama, there's still no hope for change— at least none from the pockets of his brother Barack.

Barack has, however, bestowed more than $20,000 on his racist, anti-Semite, anti-American "like family" friend, Rev. Jeremiah Wright.

The media made no point of this contrast.

Nor did the media note— as surely it would have had the players been reversed here— the stark contrast between Barack's indifference toward the sad plight of his own brother and the fact that rival John McCain and his wife had so completely changed the life of a poor little orphan girl in Bangladesh with facial disorders by providing her with costly plastic surgery and adopting her as their daughter.

"I have given some good gifts— you get some nice stuff. Here's the general rule: I give nicer stuff than I get."

℘

That's what Barack told stanch supporter Oprah Winfrey during the 2009 TV show *Christmas at the White House: An Oprah Primetime Special.*

Oprah, who had once said of him that "his tongue is dipped in the unvarnished truth," should have checked out his nose more carefully than she had checked his tongue. If Barack were Pinocchio his nose would have been zooming way out right at her.

Surely she was aware of two fiascos in which Barack's notion of presidential gift-giving had made him and our country appear tacky.

When British Prime Minister Gordon Brown visited the newly sworn-in president he was aware that Obama had selected for his Oval Office desk one made from the timbers of the *HMS Resolute* that had been a gift from Queen Victoria to President Rutherford B. Hayes– and on behalf of the people of the UK Brown proudly presented Obama with a beautiful pencil holder carved from its antislavery sister ship the *HMS Gannet*, a classy, touching choice for a gift to present to America's first black president.

And for us Barack reciprocated with: A DVD set of Hollywood movies! "Psycho" was one of them.

If you're thinking "it's the thought that counts," think about this: Brown is vision-impaired, making movies a bad gift choice. Making it worse: the cheap set of DVDs were NTSC video system used in the US and therefore not compatible with the PAL video system used for UK players.

Barack got an opportunity to try to recover some from this gift-giving embarrassment soon after when he called upon Queen Elizabeth in England– whereupon he presented Her Majesty with an iPod (it was well known that she already had one).

He first loaded it up for her– with recordings of *his* speeches and pictures of *him.*

"We are the ones we have been waiting for."

ೕ

This was a phrase Barack proclaimed– over and over – that the Obama campaign and the media pointed to as evidence of his eloquence and profundity.

"We are the ones we have been waiting for." What in the world is that supposed to mean?

Obama never explained what he meant by it. The media never asked. So, long later, we're still waiting for an explanation.

If we are the ones we have been waiting for, who has kept us waiting? Wouldn't we be the ones who kept ourselves waiting? Why would we do that?

What is most interesting about it is its source. Barack early on credited his "like family" friend and mentor Rev. Jeremiah Wright as being the source for the title of his book *The Audacity of Hope*— yet he never credited Alice Walker, author of a collection of essays titled *We Are the Ones We Have Been Waiting For*, as being the source for this meaningless line campaign rallying call of his the media found so cool.

Remember the media coverage about how this second friend and inspiration for Barack hates Catholics and Jews? About how she counts notorious cop-killers among her heroes, right up there with Fidel Castro – "If Fidel could dance, he'd be perfect!"? About her declarations that what we needed to do with Osama bin Laden was just "remind him of all the good, nonviolent things he has done'?

No one else remembers such coverage either.

The public did not like it when we learned that the man from whom Obama borrowed *The Audacity of Hope* was an anti-American, left-wing extremist nutcase. Obama did not wish to draw any attention to the fact that the woman from whom he stole *We Are The Ones We Have Been Waiting For* was just as extremist. As so often happened, the media took Barack's wish as their command.

"You know, I am a believer in...in knowing what you're doing when you apply for a job. Uh, and I think that...if I were seriously to consider running on a national ticket, I would essentially have to start now, before having served a day in the Senate.
Now there may be some people who are comfortable doing that, but I am not one of those people."

ಓ

The truly funny part of what Barack said during this television interview shortly after his election to the US Senate isn't that it turned out that he was not at all uncomfortable with what he said he would be so uncomfortable doing.

No, what he said that was so funny was that he believes in knowing what you are doing before you apply for a job doing it.

What he was sort of admitting here – think about it – is that he was not up to the job of being President of the United States.

And in time he proved that was indeed so.

"I didn't overpromise. And I didn't under-estimate how tough this was gonna be. I always believed that this was a long-term project; this wasn't a short-term project... what I understood coming in was that reversing a culture here in Washington, dominated by special interests, reversing a political culture that was dominated by polls and sound bites and 24-hour news cycle, reversing structural problems in our economy that have been building up for two decades, that was gonna take time. It was gonna take more than a year. It was gonna take more than two years. It was gonna take more than one term. Probably takes more than one president."

He didn't overpromise?

Barack may have slowed the rise of the oceans.

Barack may have begun the healing of the planet.

But no way did he overpromise.

So he asserted during a CBS News interview shortly before Christmas 2011.

Well...

What about how he was going to fix the economy for us simply by bringing a skidding halt to "the failed economic policies of the past"?

How's that "change we can believe in" been working out?

However inadvertently, isn't he really admitting that under his leadership things are not going at all well?

But, as always, Barack succeeds in his search to find an excuse.

Forget his first year in office.

Forget his second year.

So what if he and his fellow Democrats had control of not just the presidency but also both houses of Congress.

The problem – as he reveals he knew all along but just didn't get around to mentioning – is that he needs to be president longer.

Yeah, that's what the country needs.

More Barack.

But during his search for an excuse here doesn't he stumble into telling a truth?

That the solution for what ails America "probably" takes more than one president?

Not "probably"—*definitely* a president a whole lot different from Barack.

"The one thing I'm clear about is that I'd rather be a really good one-term president than a mediocre two-term president."

ॐ

Isn't Barack trying to suggest here that he is a really good president? Doesn't that raise this question: How could anyone possibly think such a thing?

His remark was in the context of a discussion with ABC News' Diane Sawyer about the very real likelihood that he will not get a second term. Why he appears to be suggesting that his having two terms means two mediocre terms while simultaneously seeming to be of a mind that his present term is better than mediocre is anyone's guess.

Barack was borrowing from one of the most famous lines of American political history, just as so many others have done.

"I'd rather be right than president," is the remark for which Henry Clay is best remembered.

Clay– Vice-President, Speaker of the House, US Senator, Secretary of State—ran for president three times, each time unsuccessfully. Unlike Barack he ran as a candidate who could point to a record of wide experience and notable achievements. There was good reason "The Great Compromiser" was chosen as the first ever person to lie in state in the United States Capitol, and it wasn't just because he's the man who introduced the Mint Julep to the Nation's Capital.

So when Henry Clay said he'd rather be right than president it was believable. When Barack Obama seems to make such a claim it's laughable.

The story goes that when Clay said "I'd rather be right than president" some wag in the audience said in a loud whisper, "Don't worry, you'll never be either."

History shows that while Clay never did get to be president he so very often got things right.

Just as history shows that while Barack did get to be president he so seldom got things right.

"I'm less interested in allocating blame than just making sure that we're taking every step we need to, to move the economy forward."

ॐ

Barack is less interested in allocating blame?

What a hoot!

Any careful and honest review of how the man approaches his duties in office will indicate that there does not seem to be anything that Barack is more interested in than in placing blame.

And it's always placed elsewhere.

It is common practice for politicians when pressed to allocate blame to fall back on the old chant that there's plenty of blame to go around, by which they acknowledge that they are, at least in some small way, partly to blame.

Not Barack. Try to think of an instant where he stepped up and shared blame for anything, even by using this "there's enough blame to go around" ploy.

No one is faster on the draw when it comes to pointing the finger of blame at someone or something else than Barack.

He once blamed his losing the Kentucky primary to Hillary Clinton on her being from "an adjacent state" when the state she represented, New York, is, of course, not adjacent to Kentucky whereas the state he represented, Illinois, is.

Admitting to being a lazy person during a December 23, 2011, television interview with Barbara Walters, he blamed not himself but Hawaii. "Probably from growing up in Hawaii and it's sunny outside."

And while Barack accepts none of the blame for the way the nation's economy has suffered so much on his watch, he has shown no hesitation to blame it on: George W. Bush, "Messy democracy," technology, the earthquake in Japan, ATM machines, oil speculators, Wall Street fat cats, Congress, the Republicans, corporations, the "Arab Spring," and just about anyone or anything else he can think of.

Blame anyone but him – that's Barack's motto.

His crock runneth over.

Barack's so full of it.

❧

"There was something stirring across the country because of what happened in Selma, Alabama, because some folks are willing to march across a bridge. So they got together and Barack Obama Jr. was born. So don't tell me I don't have a claim on Selma, Alabama. Don't tell me I'm not coming home to Selma, Alabama."

☙

Barack has never claimed he was born in a manger.

But he has claimed something about himself that rivals anything ever attributed to Jesus or to anyone else in recorded history.

To one-up fellow attendees Hillary and Bill Clinton at a March 4, 2008, event commemorating the infamous "Bloody Sunday" voting rights march in Selma, Alabama, Obama moved the audience by telling how his parents, Barack Obama, Sr. and Ann Dunham, had been so inspired by their feelings following that event that they conceived him.

The audience loved it – and it gave him a link to Selma that the Clintons, despite their long years of involvement in civil rights issues and black America politics, couldn't match.

But it was a crock.

Obama was claiming what no one else in his right mind in recorded history had ever claimed— that he was conceived *after* he was born.

Barack Obama was born on August 4, 1961.

The Selma march occurred on March 4, 1965 – almost four years later.

"Over the last 15 months, we've traveled to every corner of the United States. I've now been in 57 states. I think one left to go. Alaska and Hawaii I was not allowed to go to even though I really wanted to visit."

೮೨

Knowing how many states are in the United States of America is not a requirement for being President of the United States.

Lucky for Barack!

Check out the remarks he made during a May 8, 2008, campaign stop in Beaverton, Oregon.

Barack seems sure there are at least 57 states in the United States.

He thinks *maybe* one more.

And this is not counting Alaska and Hawaii

So...it is unclear if he thinks that the United States has 59 states or if he thinks that it has 60 states.

The correct answer is: 50.

When Republican candidate George W. Bush during his first campaign for president was unable to name the leaders of Chechnya, India and Pakistan the major media treated it as a huge story.

When Sarah Palin asked a newsman for more clarity when he asked her for her views on "the Bush doctrine," she was subjected to great ridicule, despite the fact that a) Bush had never himself referred to any "Bush doctrine" and b) the news media had itself represented more than a few different things as being "the Bush doctrine."

When presidential candidate Michelle Bachman mistakenly referred to the anniversary of Elvis Presley's death as his birthday, the news media widely reported it and treated it as some sort of major blunder, just as they did when she named the wrong town in Iowa as the birthplace of beloved American actor John Wayne.

But Barack's uncertainty about how many states are in the United States of America was not even mentioned by most of the major media.

"She's talking like she's Annie Oakley!
Hillary Clinton's out there like
she's on the duck blind every Sunday—
she's packin' a six shooter!"

ൿ

Barack got some good laughs during a primary campaign appearance in Pennsylvania in 2008 by mocking his rival Hillary Clinton's odd attempts to ingratiate herself with hunters by trying to portray herself as some outdoors woman.

She deserved to be laughed at about it.

But...

You do not hunt duck with a six-shooter.

You use a shotgun.

Barack's point that Hillary Clinton really doesn't know squat about hunting is valid.

But while making it he revealed that he doesn't either.

"They get bitter, they cling to guns or religion or antipathy toward people who aren't like them or anti-immigrant sentiment or anti-trade sentiment as a way to explain their frustrations."

❧

Pity poor ole Barack having to endure dealing with such bitter, unsophisticated people in order to run for president.

That was his campaign pitch to a group of fellow liberal elitists at a ritzy San Francisco fundraiser on April 11, 2008, speaking of the Americans who lived in small towns in Pennsylvania and the Midwest and bemoaning what he seemed to see as their reacting to the economic decline of that area of the country by clinging to things his San Francisco audience would likely find abhorrent.

These small town folks are trigger-happy and "cling to" religion because they are bitter?

Religious Americans are that way, not because they have faith in God, but because they are bitter that the area in which they live is not as prosperous as it once was?

People who hunt do so, not because they enjoy nature, the great outdoors and the challenge and camaraderie associated with hunting, but just do it because it's what bitter people like to do?

Their concerns about illegal immigration and the country's massive trade imbalance should be dismissed because all it means is that they are bitter people who don't like people who are not just like them?

Many felt that Barack's comments were, as Hillary Clinton said, "demeaning...elitist and out of touch." She added: "People don't need a president who looks down on them; they need a president who stands up for them."

"I said something that everybody knows is true," Barack shot back.

Everybody knows he spoke the truth?

Everybody?

He really believes that?

"Look, I've got two daughters. Nine years old and six years old. I am going to teach them first of all about values and morals. But if they make a mistake, I don't want them punished with a baby."

৪১

Punished? He sees a baby as a punishment?

While no sensible person would ever suggest that Barack views the two baby girls of his that his wife Michelle gave birth to as punishments, over the many years that abortion has raged as an important issue no other major political figure has ever suggested that any woman who is having a baby, including an unmarried woman, is being "punished."

Such callousness and animosity as Barack displayed in making that comment at a March 29, 2008, campaign event in Johnstown, Pennsylvania, after a woman had urged him to work against abortion, is a clue to his extremist views on abortion. He stands at the fringes on the matter of abortion, far more extreme than even most ultra-liberals.

He is an advocate for partial birth abortion, a procedure whereby a baby, while being delivered alive, is killed by driving a spike into its head and vacuum sucking its brains out. The late liberal Democratic US Senator Daniel Patrick Moynihan called partial birth abortion what it really is: 'infanticide."

As a state senator, Obama crusaded to prevent Illinois from passing an anti-infanticide measure protecting a baby who survives an abortion from being allowed to die by withholding nourishment and medical care. He chaired the committee that killed that bill. Later, a virtually identical federal measure became law, passing the House on voice vote and passing the Senate unanimously. Even such ultra-liberals as Teddy Kennedy and Barbara Boxer spoke out in favor of it. Barack now says he would have voted for that federal bill, claiming it to be different from the bill he had opposed– a claim that is a complete crock.

"I consider it part of my responsibility as President of the United States to fight against negative stereotypes of Islam wherever they appear."

ℬ

The Constitution of the United States enumerates the responsibilities of the President of the United States.

If you are President of the United States you should know what they are.

If you are President of the United States and you do not know what they are, you should get out a copy of the Constitution and read it or, if that's too much of a bother, get one of your advisors to explain to you just what your responsibilities as president happen to be.

Not included among them is any responsibility to fight against negative stereotypes of Islam – or, for that matter, any other religion.

Of course the Muslim audience listening to Barack Obama's speech in Cairo on June 4, 2009, can be forgiven if they believed him. How should they know?

But the President of the United States should know better.

"If a family care physician works with his or her patient to help them lose weight, modify diet, monitors whether they're taking their medications in a timely fashion, they might get reimbursed a pittance. But if that same diabetic ends up getting their foot amputated, that's $30,000, $40,000, $50,000— immediately the surgeon is reimbursed."

ॐ

We know— because he publicly said so— that Barack is under the impression that one of his responsibilities as President of the United States is to "fight against negative stereotypes of Islam," but remarks such as these that he made about physicians —during a town hall meeting held in Portsmouth, New Hampshire, while he was president— show that to advance his argument for government dominance of health care he has no qualms about making a personal contribution to some silly stereotypical portrayal of doctors as greedy people who are in medicine just for the money.

He makes it sound as if doctors would prefer that patients not prevent serious disease because the worse off the patient gets the greater the possibility of more bucks for the doc.

In his smearing of doctors in order to try to advance his political agenda he demonstrated a blatant disregard for the truth.

The surgeon he portrays as so anxious to amputate so he can "immediately" pocket "$30,000, $40,000, $50,000" would be reimbursed nowhere remotely near that amount, in fact, but a small fraction of what Barack claimed.

The truth is, reimbursement for a leg amputation runs from a low of around $400 to a high of around $1,200. And that figure includes not just the surgery but also post-operation follow through for a three-month period during which most patients require at least three additional consultations with the physician.

We have no way of knowing if Barack said what he said because he was just ignorant or if he deliberately lied. What is certainly obvious, however, is that for Barack to represent himself as someone knowledgeable about health care is a total crock.

"So if they're looking— and you come in and you've got a bad sore throat, or your child has a bad sore throat or has repeated sore throats, the doctor may look at the reimbursement system and say to himself, you know what, I make a lot more money if I take this kid's tonsils out."

౭ర

There he goes again!

This comment made by him during a presidential news conference in July 2009 demonstrates once again that, while he is under the illusion that he has a responsibility as president to fight against negative stereotypes of Islam anywhere they might pop up, he loves to pop off to try to sell us on his highly negative stereotype of doctors as money-grabbers.

Be wary of trusting your doctor to deal with your kid's sore throat because when he sees that sore throat he's probably looking at it as an excuse to perform some unnecessary work on your child so he can pocket some extra money. Isn't that what Barack is suggesting here?

You can't trust doctors – so trust Barack with the nation's health care system.

What Barack always prescribes is a big dose of Barack— and it never comes with one of those warnings about adverse side-effects.

"So for example, I closed Guantanamo. That was the right thing to do"

ॐ

Got that?

Guantanamo is closed.

Barack closed it.

So he says.

Said this on March 19, 2009.

But it wasn't closed.

OK, what he probably really meant to say when he said this is that in one of his first official acts as president he had signed an Executive Order to close the Guantanamo Bay Detention Facility within one year.

He had issued that Executive Order on January 22, with much fanfare in the Oval Office, which meant it would be closed down by not later than 22 January 2010.

And as he was doing it he boasted that he was already fulfilling a campaign promise:

"As President, I will close Guantanamo."

He first made this promise in a speech delivered on August 2, 2007. He repeated his promise often and loudly throughout the 2008 campaign.

But— check it out— the Guantanamo Bay Detention Facility was never closed.

Barack's self-imposed deadline for closing came and went and then, on March 7, 2011, he got around to issuing another Executive Order, an order that, as the Washington *Post* put it, "will create a formal system of indefinite detention for those held at the U.S. military prison at Guantanamo Bay" and "all but cements Guantanamo Bay's continuing role."

Which raises the question: If George W. Bush was so wrong to permit the existence of the Guantanamo Bay Detention Center and Barack was so right to promise to close it, why did Barack belatedly decide to follow Bush's lead?

"Well, I should say at the outset that 'Skip' Gates is a friend, so I may be a little biased here. I don't know all the facts... Now, I don't know, not having been there and not seeing all the facts, what role race played in that. But I think it's fair to say, number one, any of us would be pretty angry; number two, that the Cambridge Police acted stupidly ...blacks and Hispanics are picked up more frequently and often time for no cause casts suspicion even when there is good cause."

ॐ

After establishing that he does not know the facts about a particular incident, Barack promptly proceeds to assert that those facts would make anyone angry and that they prove stupidity; he also seems to suggest a strong possibility racial prejudice was involved here.

When the Cambridge, Massachusetts, police department received a 911 call reporting a possible house break-in, the responding police officer, who had reason to believe that he might be coming upon a crime in progress, asked a man he spotted inside to please step out. When the man whom he thought to be an intruder responded, "No, I will not," the police officer rightly insisted. Next, Professor Henry Gates, who is black, proceeded to berate Sergeant James Crowley, who is white, to the point where normal procedure calls for the officer to handcuff and arrest the abusing suspect for disorderly conduct.

Turns out that Gates locked himself out and broke into his own house. Neither the neighbor who reported the break-in nor the officer who responded knew this. Charges could still be pressed against him because of his conduct, but they were dropped.

That the President of the United States would be asked about such a minor matter is weird.

Weirder still— and bewildering— is that a president would be so lacking in sound judgment and common sense as to insert himself into such a minor matter rather than simply decline to comment.

Confessing that you have no idea what you are talking about and then proceeding to pontificate at length about a subject about which you admit knowing nothing meets the textbook definition of a total crock.

No question about it, someone acted stupidly here— but that someone was not a member of the Cambridge, Massachusetts, police department.

"There are those who say we cannot afford to invest in science. That support for research is somehow a luxury at a moment defined by necessities. I fundamentally disagree. Science is more essential for our prosperity, our security, our health, our environment, and our quality of life than it has ever been."

Who?

Who is it who is saying that we cannot afford to invest in science? Who?

Why doesn't Barack name names, say exactly who one or more of these people are to whom he is referring here rather than just saying "there are those"?

Because straw men don't have names, that's why.

"Straw man" is a common trick used in argument to try to fool an audience by misrepresenting the position of your debate opponent by replacing what his position is with something else, usually something with some superficial similarity, and then attacking that other position as if it were the one in question.

It's a logical fallacy that fools a lot of people a lot of the time.

In this case, the argument at hand was not if we should "invest in science" but if it was prudent to spend money on all the things that he would like to see money spent on and to the exact extent in each instance that he would prefer, only some of which could be considered to fall under the category of science.

The name for this shifty tactic is commonly believed to have been derived from the practice in military training exercise in which an attack is mounted against a pretend person made of straw rather than against the real thing. It may also have come into use in reference to a practice of centuries ago in which a man standing outside a courthouse with a straw in his shoe signaled his availability to be a false witness.

When it comes to avoiding tough facts by instead attacking straw men, few can match Barack. He's a true Sultan of Sophistry.

"It's only right that we ask everyone to pay their fair share."

৪৩

Fred J. Eckert

Ask?

Government doesn't "ask" you to give it money. It forces you to.

The power that government possesses to tax is just that, a power – the power to require that you do as ordered and surrender money to it. To get you to part with money government does not rely on the power of persuasion, it relies on its power to punish.

But Barack repeatedly says "ask" when speaking of imposing requirements. Saying "ask" in such a context is, of course, a crock.

If he is just "asking," shouldn't you be able to decline? Obviously. And since you cannot, use of that word is just more linguistic trickery from the mouth of the Sultan of Sophistry.

Notice how Barack managed a double crock in that sentence.

He's just "asking" that we pay our "fair share."

Fair to whom?

Barack frequently uses "fair share" to suggest that those persons currently turning over to government a disproportionately *low* proportion of their income— or even none— are somehow unfairly victimized by those person currently turning over a disproportionately *high* proportion.

What exactly is the "fair share" of a citizen's income to which government should be able to lay claim?

Barack never says.

And a fawning media never bothers to ask him this obvious question.

*"We used to have the best infrastructure
in the world here in America.
We're the country that built the
intercontinental railroad."*

ဆ

We built the intercontinental railroad?

Bet you didn't even know that.

Which continents does our intercontinental railroad run to and from?

Does it connect North America with Europe?

Does it connect North America with Asia?

Does it connect us with Australia?

Africa?

Antarctica?

Or does it not run over or under the oceans and only connect us with South America?

How did we do it?

When did we do it?

Imagine that.

Imagine how we missed hearing about it.

Imagine what the news media coverage would have been had a George W. Bush or a Sarah Palin or any conservative said this.

"God's grace, and the compassion and decency of the American people, is expressed through the men and women like Corpsman Brossard."

જી

When Barack related to us a story about this member of the US military he quoted the words spoken by *corpse* man Brossard.

He said it was a *corpse* man speaking.

Simple slip of the tongue? Not likely.

He referred to Brossard as a *corpse* man not just once, not just twice, but three times.

There you have it:

On one hand, the Obama campaign and the fawning media portray Barack as a great intellect with compelling command of the language.

On the other hand, as Barack reads from his teleprompter he reveals— three times— that he does not know that the "p" in *corpsman* is silent.

Perhaps the folks loading up Barack's teleprompter should take some extra time and spoon feed him even more by spelling out his words phonetically.

Again:

Imagine what the news media coverage would have been had a George W. Bush or a Sarah Palin or any conservative said this.

"(Magic Johnson has) an infections enthusiasm for life."

&

An *infections* enthusiasm for life?

In his remarks during a White House ceremony welcoming National Basketball Association (NBA) champions, the Los Angeles Lakers, and Lakers Hall of Famer Earvin "Magic" Johnson, Jr., Barack shared with us that "Magic" has an "infections" enthusiasm for life.

Had Barack wished to speak correct English, the word he should have used, of course, is *infectious*.

But neither *infections* nor *infectious* was a prudent choice here since the one thing anyone who has ever heard of "Magic" Johnson is almost sure to associate with him is that the reason he retired from playing professional basketball is because he has the infectious disease known as HIV.

Again:

Imagine what the news media coverage would have been had a George W. Bush or a Sarah Palin or any conservative said this.

"When I meet with world leaders, whether it's in Europe or here in Asia..."

ॐ

Time for a geography lesson for Barack?

It's a safe bet that mocking comments of that sort would have been the norm and would have drawn wide attention rather than being ignored had this comment at this place been made by a George W. Bush or a Sarah Palin or some conservative rather than by Barack Obama.

But, the media being so keen on keeping up the double standard, Barack was given a pass.

Barack said this in Honolulu.

Honolulu is in Hawaii.

Hawaii is in the United States of America.

The United States of America is *not* in Asia.

"We all remember Abraham Lincoln as the leader who saved our union. Founder of the Republican Party..."

જી

When Barack appeared before a joint session of Congress on September 8, 2011, and repeatedly admonished Congress to swiftly pass yet another massive stimulus spending measure which he without even laughing referred to as the "American Jobs Act," he, his fellow Democrats and their allies in the media seemed to view it as of little interest that no such legislation even existed.

Something will be coming along. So pass it – quick.

And in a maladroit attempt to appear bi-partisan, he heaped praise upon a great Republican president, Abraham Lincoln – "a leader who looked to the future...leaders of both parties have followed the example he set."

Now consider this report from *TIME* Magazine: *He gives a good speech, but he's loose with the facts. He called Abraham Lincoln the 'founder' of the Republican Party. Nope. Lincoln was not the founder of the party; he wasn't even the first Republican nominee (John Fremont was, in 1856). Lincoln was, of course, the first Republican to be elected president.*

That slap was against former Governor Mike Huckabee about a speech he made in 2008. It was written by bureau chief Jay Carney, who was Obama's press secretary when Barack made the same mistake.

Hardly earth shaking, yet you can imagine the media brouhaha that would have erupted had George W. Bush made such a gaffe while speaking before a joint session of Congress. But look at the transcript of Obama's remarks as published by taxpayer-subsidized PBS:

We all remember Abraham Lincoln as the leader who saved our Union. But in the middle of a Civil War...

Barack's gaff second sentence—*Founder of the Republican Party*— was deliberately omitted by PBS.

Think media bias is just a myth?

*Imagine a President who will
curb spending, cut programs,
bring the budget deficit and the
national debt under control,
and give us cheap health care, too—
as he ends business as usual by beating
back the special interests and giving us a
truly transparent government
that we can trust.*

Or was he just Baracking us?

"Today I am pledging to cut the deficit we inherited by half by the end of my first term in office."

☜☞

Yet another empty promise.

When Barack made this pledge to the American people only a couple weeks after taking office, he was simultaneously pushing for major new government spending sprees certain to increase the gap between income and outgo in both the short and long terms and turning a blind eye to cutting spending.

A financial markets collapse is a far different creature from the usual vicissitudes of business cycle swings because it can cause both unusually sharp uptick movements and unusually sharp downs as well in the deficit position, making it incredibly difficult to accurately assess where the deficit stands at any given point during a fiscal year as opposed to measuring beginning and end— and Barack was well along into a fiscal year when he made this comment.

Therefore...

Using one set of Congressional Budget Office figures one could claim that the deficit at the end of his term *might* be just under $1 trillion, down from $1.2 trillion.

Using another set of CBO figures one could claim that it *might* be in the $600-$900 billion dollar range, up from $458 billion.

As for the promise that it will be cut in half?

Any way you look at it, that's a crock.

*"I refuse to leave our children with a debt
that they cannot repay. And that means
taking responsibility right now,
in this administration, for getting our
spending under control."*

&

Before Barack took responsibility "right now" in February, 2009, the Congressional Budget Office estimate of the national debt was: $10.626 trillion.

Three years into his four year term it topped $15 trillion.

By the end of his term it will be more than 50% greater than it was the day he took office.

The national debt rose faster under Barack than under any other president in America's history.

The CBO estimates that— thanks largely to his policies— it will top $26 trillion by 2020 unless there is a serious and dramatic course correction.

So much for his notion of taking responsibility, getting spending under control and refusing to burden the next generation with massive debt.

"In these challenging times, when we are facing both rising deficits and a sinking economy, budget reform is not an option. It is an imperative. We cannot sustain a system that bleeds billions of taxpayer dollars on programs that have outlived their usefulness, or exist solely because of the power of politicians, lobbyists, or interest groups. We simply cannot afford it. This isn't about big government or small government. It's about building a smarter government that focuses on what works. That is why I will ask my new team to think anew and act anew to meet our new challenges...We will go through our federal budget– page by page, line by line– eliminating those programs we don't need, and insisting that those we do operate in a sensible cost-effective way."

Isn't it great that all those programs we didn't need are now gone?

Isn't it great that the ones we do need – only ones still around, right?— are now being operated in such a sensible cost-effective way?

How did Barack do it?

Must have been the way he said he'd do it, the way he explained to the country that he would when he addressed the American people only a few weeks after taking office.

Guess he did it by all that page-by-page, line-by-line hard-working attention to detail that he managed to get in when he wasn't out on the golf course or away on yet another extended vacation.

Right?

"When I'm president, I will go line by line to make sure that we are not spending money unwisely."

&

"I'll order a top-to-bottom audit of government spending and eliminate government programs that don't work."

&

"Now, many of these plans will cost money, which is why I've laid out how I'll pay for every dime— by closing corporate loopholes and tax havens that don't help America grow. But I will also go through the federal budget, line by line, eliminating programs that no longer work and making the ones we do need work better and cost less— because we cannot meet twenty-first century challenges with a twentieth century bureaucracy."

How many times does he have to tell us? What more can we expect of him?

By now Barack has probably finished his top to bottom audit, closed all those corporate loopholes and tax havens and also gone through the federal budget line by line, eliminating those bad programs that don't work and making the good ones work better. He's made sure we're not spending any money unwisely.

Right?

Quick, name one of the federal programs he's eliminated.

Quick, name one that's now less costly than it was before and running better, too.

And while you're at it, take a stab at answering this question:

If he's done this, just like he said he would, how is it that federal spending is expanding and the deficit and debt are growing?

"The problem is, is that the way Bush has done it over the last eight years is to take out a credit card from the Bank of China in the name of our children, driving up our national debt from $5 trillion for the first 42 presidents— Number 43 added $4 trillion by his lonesome, so that we now have over $9 trillion of debt that we are going to have to pay back—$30,000 for every man, woman and child.
That's irresponsible. It's unpatriotic."

৪৩

Calling President George W. Bush irresponsible because of the spending policies he endorsed and espoused, as Barack did during remarks he made on July 3, 2008, while campaigning in Fargo, North Dakota, is, of course, a perfectly legitimate charge to make when claiming that you want to see policy changes that would curb out-of-control government deficit and debt.

But calling Bush unpatriotic?

When the McCain campaign expressed wonder about Barack's seeming to have experienced no discomfort while so closely associating himself with a lineup of people well known for their hatred of America, such as Rev. Jeremiah Wright and the unrepentant domestic terrorist Bill Ayers, didn't Obama indignantly complain that they were questioning his patriotism?

Don't a number of Democratic politicians make it a practice as their rebuttal to legitimate criticism to indignantly complain that their patriotism is being questioned?

Don't the media routinely join in echoing the suggestion that some of the criticism of these Democrats amounts to questioning their patriotism?

And don't these particular Democrats and their media allies do this even though the criticism levied against them did not, in fact, mention or suggest any issue of patriotism?

If Barack thinks it was "unpatriotic" of Bush to advance policies that led to such an increase in deficit and debt, then by Barack's own reasoning doesn't the fact that the policies that he has advanced, which have led to a significantly greater increase in deficit and debt than Bush's, make Barack even more unpatriotic than Bush?

"The fact that we are here today to debate raising America's debt limit is a sign of leadership failure. It is a sign that the U.S. Government can't pay its own bills. It is a sign that we now depend on ongoing financial assistance from foreign countries to finance our Government's reckless fiscal policies. Increasing America's debt weakens us domestically and internationally. Leadership means that 'the buck stops here.' Instead, Washington is shifting the burden of bad choices today onto the backs of our children and grandchildren. America has a debt problem and a failure of leadership. Americans deserve better."

That's what Barack said on the floor of the US Senate on March 16, 2006, in urging his colleagues to join with him in voting against raising the debt ceiling to $9 trillion.

Five years later, on April 14, 2011, asked to square his plea against raising the debt ceiling with his practice as president of advocating to increase it far greater, Barack dismissed his own remarks as just a crock: "That was just an example of a new Senator, you know, making what is a political vote, as opposed to doing what was important for the country."

If, as he admits, he voted against that debt ceiling increase in 2006 while feeling that in doing so he was failing to do the right thing for the country, then what about the debt ceiling increase votes that came before the Senate in 2007 and 2008?

Did Barack change, do what he thinks is the important and right thing to do for the country, and in 2007 and 2008 vote for the debt ceiling increases? No, in 2007 and 2008 he did not even bother to vote on this important matter.

Nice to quote that old line that "the buck stops here" while admonishing others, but then why later just pass the buck yourself?

If it was "a failure of leadership" not to solve the debt problem when someone else was president, what is it when Barack is president?

And isn't his talking one way and acting in the opposite way both solid evidence that what he says is a crock and also proof positive indeed that "Americans deserve better"?

"This plan will save or create over three million jobs— almost all of them in the private sector."

ଊଠ

You can never say with certainty how many jobs a given government spending program will create.

You can only estimate. That is, guess.

As to the matter of how many jobs a given government program might save – that is, prevent from being eliminated– that would not just be a guess, that would be a *wild* guess.

Not until Barack did the federal government pretend that it was credible to correctly count number of jobs saved.

So why does Barack do it?

Because it is so easy to make numbers look good for you if all you have to do is make them up.

How can you prove that a job was or was not saved? You can't.

But even if you play the "created and saved" game and accept the Obama Administration's very highest numbers claimed, the cost per job "created or saved" because of the stimulus spending bill, *The American Recovery and Reinvestment Act of 2009*, comes to just under a quarter-of-a-million dollars— again, that's *per-job*.

If instead of using their most rosy estimates (guesses) you use their lower end one then the cost *per-job* "created or saved" comes to just under $600,000.

Washington may be broke – but it's not cheap!

"We measure progress by how many people can find a job that pays the mortgage; whether you can put a little extra money away at the end of each month so you can someday watch your child receive her college diploma."

৪৩

Not a bad measure, right?

Thus:

By the measurement standard that Barack says he goes by, we're making progress when more people are able to find jobs that enable them to pay their bills and set some extra money aside, correct?

So how are things measuring up under Barack?

*"I will cut taxes— cut taxes— for 95%
of all working families. Because in an
economy like this, the last thing we
should do is raise taxes on
the middle-class."*

ॐ

*"If you have a job, pay taxes and
make less than $200,000 a year,
you'll get a tax cut."*

ॐ

*"I will eliminate capital gains taxes for
the small businesses and the startups
that will create the high-wage, high-tech
jobs of tomorrow."*

So...

95% of working families in America are now paying less in taxes today than when Barack made this promise?

No.

Not true.

But every job-holding, tax-paying American earning under $200,000-a-year got a tax cut, right?

No.

Not true.

But at least the capital gains taxes on small businesses and startups have been eliminated, right?

No.

Not true either.

It was all a crock?

Exactly.

*"For the sake of our economy, our
security, and the future of our planet,
I will set a clear goal as President:
in ten years, we will finally end our
dependence on oil from the Middle East."*

❧

Let's be fair and give Barack credit for knowing that it is good to have goals. "A clear goal"? All the better.

With three of the ten years for reaching that goal having ticked by, let's check out any indications suggesting that Barack is on track to finally ending our dependence on oil from the Middle East.

Are we at long last tapping into all the oil potential just off our shores? What about all that untapped oil right here in Alaska? Are we tapping into it at long last?

What about getting more oil from our good friend and neighbor Canada, whose oil reserves are second only to those of Saudi Arabia? Instead of giving Canada any incentive to pipe crude oil from Alberta to British Columbia for refinement there to ship on to China, we made certain that the Keystone Pipeline will be carrying all that Canadian crude down to the United States for refinement here, right?

What about taking full advantage of the latest technique – hydraulic fracturing – for harvesting oil and natural gas? What about nuclear power?

Forget all that. Barack had a better idea: Just shower hundreds of millions of taxpayer dollars on the "green energy" companies of his campaign donors.

Such as Solyndra.

So what if the Office of Management & Budget complained that they had not yet had "sufficient time to do our due diligence reviews"? So what if that Department of Energy guy behind the push to ignore such precaution was a Barack fundraiser married to a partner in the law firm representing Solyndra for this $535 million taxpayer loan guarantee?

And so what if the usual practice got reversed so that instead of taxpayers having first claim on any recovered monies instead Barack's political contributor friends moved to the front of the line?

"When you give a tax break to working families who are struggling, they will spend it on buying a new coat for the kids, or making sure that they get that car repaired that they use to get to work. When you give it to the wealthier families, they just put it away somewhere, and so it doesn't circulate in the economy."

&

Rich people cannot be trusted to spend money? That's what Barack seems to be suggesting here.

Normal folks who come into some extra cash will spend it, but wealthier folks will "just put it away somewhere"?

Actually, it is a pretty well-known fact— among not just professional economists but nearly everyone else in the world as well— that wealthier people do buy coats and do care for their cars.

Yes, there probably are some eccentric wealthy people who would put money away under a mattress or whatever, just as there are some not-so-wealthy eccentrics who would do the same dumb thing.

Barack himself is a very wealthy person, so maybe he should have asked himself if that's what he would do with extra dollars.

Or would he instead, as all but the dumbest do, make purchases or invest that money?

Maybe buy stock in some companies that would use the money to grow, thereby creating new job opportunities?

Maybe buy bonds, thereby helping enable such economic activity as building things such as schools?

If you are looking for an explanation of how Barack was able achieve such spectacular success in taking a bad economy and making it far, far worse, look no further than examples like this of his muddle-mindedness when it comes to any understanding of basic economic behavior.

"This economic crisis began as a financial crisis, when banks and financial institutions took huge, reckless risks in pursuit of quick profits and massive bonuses."

☙

Is that a fact?

No. The simple answer is that there is no simple answer.

Suggesting it was all just a simple case of manipulation by greedy Wall Street bankers working the system, taking unfair advantage of unsuspecting homeowners and investors, is demagogic nonsense.

The very people who after the collapse rushed in to decry banks taking reckless risks were people of the Left who had forced such taking of reckless risk by making the alternative to doing so the threat of serious penalty by the federal government.

Their complaint that banks were not taking great enough risks on loans had led first to the Carter-era *Community Investment Act* and then ongoing pressure to keep up the risk from the federal Department of Housing and Urban Renewal which directed the government sponsored enterprises Fannie Mae and Freddie Mac to devote a high percentage of loans— up to 50%— to sub-prime mortgages.

The idea of "affordable housing" became trying to entice as many people as possible into housing debt they could not afford, thereby ultimately inviting a mortgage market catastrophe.

When the George W. Bush Administration expressed alarm and called for checks against the Fannie and Freddie excesses, liberal Democrats, led by Senator Christopher Dodd and Congressman Barney Frank, prevented it.

The deposed head of Fannie Mae, Franklin Raines, pocketed some $90 million on his way out. He became— here's a funny one— a housing adviser for Barack's campaign. And Barack became the number two beneficiary of Fannie Mae campaign donations, closely following Senator Chris Dodd.

"We have the chance to tell all those corporate lobbyists that the days of them setting the agenda in Washington are over...
I don't take a dime of their money, and when I am president, they won't find a job in my White House."

ಬಿ

Not a dime did he take from corporate lobbyists?

That's just flat-out deceptive.

Examine the reports covering financial contributions to Barack's campaign for president and the record shows that during that campaign, as was the case during prior political campaigns of his as well, lots and lots of the money flowing into the Obama for President coffers came from, sometimes in a roundabout way— surprise!— corporate lobbyists.

And from union lobbyists and other lobbyists, too.

That is neither illegal nor unusual. What is unusual is for a candidate to make such a blatantly false claim that he does not do what all the others do when there is such clear and compelling proof that this is a not true and that proof is so readily available.

While the policies he pursued as president have pretty effectively prevented millions of other Americans who were looking for a job from finding one, try as he might Barack was not able to keep lobbyists from finding jobs in his White House— despite his having complete power to do so.

Ex-lobbyists have from the very first days of his administration filled a number of key positions in Barack's White House, just as they do throughout the departments and agencies to which he makes appointments.

Barack has signed waiver after waiver authorizing noncompliance with his promised unwavering policy of no-lobbyist-need-apply.

"When there's a bill that ends up on my desk as president, you the public will have five days to look on line and find out what's in it before I sign it so that you know what your government is doing."

☙

"When there's a tax bill being debated in Congress you will know the name of the corporations that would benefit and how much money they would get."

☙

"We will put every corporate tax break and every pork barrel project online for every American to see. You will know who asked for them."

☙

"When there are meetings between lobbyists and a government agency, we'll put as many of those meetings as possible online for every American to watch."

Time for a little quiz:

Name which ones of those promises that Barack has kept and which ones he has not kept.

It's a trick question.

He hasn't kept any of them.

Sounded nice when he was saying it.

So did:

"No more secrecy...That's the commitment I make to you as president."

And..

"When I'm president, meetings where laws are written will be more open to the public."

And...

"I'll make our government open and transparent so that anyone can insure that our business is the people's business."

None of it is true.

It was all just a crock?

You got it!

To be on C-SPAN,
Or not to be on C-SPAN.

or

Now you C-SPAN it,
Now you don't.

Saga of a serial crock.

"When we are negotiating for that plan, we're going to have C-SPAN on and you will see who is compromising the American people's interest. This will all be televised on C-SPAN. Broadcasting those negotiations on C-SPAN. I'm going to do it on C-SPAN. On C-SPAN. On C-SPAN."

৪৩

"...not negotiating behind closed doors but bringing all parties together and broadcasting those negotiations on C-SPAN so that the American people can see what the choices are."

You get his drift, right?

Barack was promising us that if he became president the negotiations on any health care reform would be out in the open for everyone to see because he would see to it that they would be broadcast on television on C-SPAN.

Could the promise possibly be more explicit?

Could anyone possibly manage to repeat "C-SPAN" so many times in such a short amount of time?

During a CNN debate in January 2008, Barack explained to his fellow candidates for the Democratic nomination and to the American people what would be different about how he would conduct health care reform negotiations if he became president— he would be broadcasting them on C-SPAN

Promise.

"We'll have the negotiations televised on C-SPAN. The people can see who is making arguments on behalf of their constituents and who are making arguments on behalf of the drug companies or the insurance companies."

ಇ

"So I'll put forward my plan, but what I'll say is: Look, if you have better ideas I'm happy to listen to them. But all this will be done in public in front of the people."

ಇ

"Here's the thing: We're going to do all these negotiations on C-SPAN. So the American people will be able to watch these negotiations."

ಇ

"These negotiations will be on C-SPAN and so the public will be part of the conversation and will see the choices that are being made."

There's the thing!

Don't worry about what might happen during the negotiations over a radical overhaul of America's health care system.

It'll all going to be out in the open for all of us to observe every step of the way.

Right there on C-SPAN.

He promises it.

Said so while campaigning in Florida.

Promised again while campaigning in Virginia.

You'll see it happening because it'll all be right there in front of the people.

Promised again while campaigning in Indiana.

Promised it again and again and again – in campaign speeches, in debating his opponents and in media interviews.

How many times does Barack have to tell us?

"I respect what the Clintons tried to do in 1993 in moving health reform forward. But they made one really big mistake. And that is they took all their people and all their experts into a room and then they closed the door. We will work on this process publicly. It'll be on C-SPAN. It'll be streaming over the net."

৵

"We will have a public process for forming this plan. It'll be televised on C-SPAN. I can't guarantee it'll be exciting so not everybody's going to be watching. But it will be transparent and accountable to the American people."

Barack wouldn't be making any big mistakes when it comes to handling health care reform.

Not like the Clintons did.

No, he learned from their big mistake.

None of that sneaky secretive stuff when he's president.

Everything out in public.

See it all on C-SPAN.

Watch it streaming on the internet.

And give Barack credit for some candor and honesty.

While campaigning in New Hampshire, he leveled with the American people and told us that, while he indeed guaranteed that all the negotiations over health care reform would be open to public viewing over C-Span, he could not guarantee that it would make for exciting television viewing.

He even said that he could not guarantee that everybody's going to be watching.

But, come to think of it, he did in the end actually find a way to guarantee that "not everybody's going to be watching."

Keep following this little saga to learn how.

*"One of my jobs as president
will be to guide this process
so that it's an honest process."*

৪৩

"An honest process" is not a phrase likely to pop up in accounts describing what occurred during the health care reform negotiations.

Truth be told, throughout the entire health care reform negotiations process Barack was more an onlooker than a guide; he followed rather than led, leaving fellow Democrats Senate Majority Leader Harry Reid and House Speaker Nancy Pelosi to present him with a package that was for him, as it was for the rest of Americans, to a very large extent a surprise package.

What most people seem to remember about the process are things such as the hundreds of millions of dollars recklessly tossed around in deals known as the "Louisiana Purchase" and the "Cornhusker Kickback."

And the fact that neither Barack nor anyone in either the Senate or the House admit to having read the bill that was being voted into law.

Voting for whatever might be included among 2,000 pages you haven't bothered to read meets the definition of buying a pig in a poke.

"We have to pass the bill so that you can find out what is in it," Speaker of the House Nancy Pelosi explained to us.

Though many thought it should be taken as such, strictly speaking Pelosi's explanation did not in and of itself constitute a medically acceptable diagnosis of brain dead.

"This is what change looks like," Barack proclaimed when it was over.

Remember what a change it was – "Change you can believe in" -- to be able to see for yourself what an honest process Barack was leading just by turning on C-SPAN?

No one else does either.

"Probably should have."

&

Thus replied Barack when a high school student asked him why he had not kept his promise to have health care reform negotiations broadcasted on television on C-SPAN.

Obama had accurately predicted that "not everybody's going to be watching."

And he had suggested that the reason why "not everybody" would watch was because such viewing is not exciting.

But, of course, a high school student could easily figure out what the news media was so careful not to notice and report – that the reason "not everybody" – that is, nobody – watched was because: the promise was a lie.

Never— not while he was running for president, not after he became president— did Barack ask C-SPAN to televise the health care reform negotiations.

And when C-SPAN asked to, it was rebuffed.

Barack said that it would happen without ever even asking.

Perhaps he was under the impression that C-SPAN is a governmental operation rather than private and could be told, not asked.

The fawning mainstream news media took the attitude that if he said it would be, then it would be.

So they never bothered to ask Barack if he had asked C-SPAN if they would agree to do so.

And they never bothered to ask C-SPAN either.

You just don't question when your bias is to blindly follow.

"Look, I made that commitment and I probably should have put it on C-SPAN, although one of the tricky things is trying to figure out, well, if it is on C-SPAN, are people actually going to be saying what they think about trying to get the bill done or is everybody going to be posturing to say things that sound good for the camera."

৪৩

Fred J. Eckert

There. He admits it. He lied.

But while we cannot depend on Barack to speak the truth, one thing we can always depend on him for is being able to think of an excuse.

All those times he was telling cheering audiences about how great it would be when he puts the health care reform negotiations on C-SPAN it never once occurred to him to mention any "tricky things to figure out"?

Apparently not.

Never once occurred to him to mention that if it was all on C-SPAN there was a possibility of political posturing?

Apparently not.

Only after the health care reform negotiations were over and done with did it occur to him to mention that some people might just "say things that sound good for the camera"?

Duh!

You mean like he had done every time he lied on camera by promising to put the health care negotiations on C-SPAN?

Birds of a feather:
Barack's flock is scary.

ಊ

"Did I know him to be an occasionally fierce critic of American domestic and foreign policy? Of course.
Did I ever hear him make remarks that could be considered controversial while I sat in church? Yes.
Did I strongly disagree with many of his political views? Absolutely— just as I'm sure many of you have heard remarks from your pastors, priests, or rabbis with which you strongly disagreed."

଼

"This is a guy who lives in my neighborhood, who's a professor of English in Chicago, who I know and who I have not received some official endorsement from. He's not someone who I exchange ideas from on a regular basis. And the notion that somebody who engaged in detestable acts 40 years ago when I was eight years old somehow reflects on me and my values doesn't make much sense."

Barack and his allies in the news media brushed off as totally insignificant his association with persons such as the racist, anti-Semitic, anti-American Rev. Jeremiah Wright and the unrepentant domestic terrorist and co-founder of the communist Weather Underground William "Bill" Ayers.

Not so fast.

The sort of persons with whom one chooses to associate, especially closely and over a prolonged period of time, offers some insight into the person opting to make the association and is a good indicator of the type of persons with whom he would be likely to associate in the future.

It was nothing but unfair "guilt by association" to suggest that Barack's association with such despicable persons as Wright and Ayer raised any questions— that was the message put forth by Barack and his campaign. The media fully accepted and then aggressively promoted this absurd assertion.

You cannot hold Barack responsible for the things that Wright and Ayers say and do, went the defense of his choosing to have associated with them.

But that was an attacking-the-straw-man defense, pleading that you were not doing what you were not being accused of doing.

No one ever said Barack's association with Wright and Ayers makes him guilty of their offenses.

But it does make him guilty of incredibly poor judgment.

Evaluating if a candidate possesses judgment sufficiently sound to entrust with the office of President of the United States is an obligation of every good citizen— so concrete evidence of such poor judgment on the part of Barack as to want to associate with the likes of Wright and Ayers is – and should be – a serious issue meriting serious discussion and debate. It is not a matter that should be lightly tossed aside and dismissed as inconsequential.

In their desire to play a supporting role in the Obama campaign as opposed to adhering to sound journalistic standards to try to serve the public interest by seeking truth and examining any political candidate's words and deeds with some healthy skepticism, the media permitted Obama to get away with fabrications and distortions about his problematic associations.

"Permitted" is putting it mildly. They acted as accomplices. They blessed his escaping proper scrutiny.

When the public caught a glimpse of Jeremiah Wright, the cult-figure pastor Barack called "like family" and had for some 20 years turned to as his spiritual advisor, selected to marry him and baptize his children and from whom he had borrowed the title of his campaign book, suddenly there was some very serious concern about the candidate.

Small wonder considering what people were seeing Wright saying in videos posted on *YouTube*, such as:

- "The government gives them the drugs, builds bigger prisons, passes a three-strike law and then wants us to sing 'God Bless America,' No, no, no, God da*n America ...God da*n America for treating our citizens as less than human."

- "The government lied about inventing the HIV virus as a means of genocide against people of color. The government lied."

- "America is still the number one killer in the world."

And in his sermon on the Sunday after 9/11, he said that the United States brought that al'Qaeda terrorist attack upon itself, just a case of our chickens coming home to roost:

- "We bombed Hiroshima, we bombed Nagasaki, and we nuked far more than the thousands in New York and the Pentagon, and we never batted an eye. We have supported state terrorism against the Palestinians and black South Africans, and now we are indignant because the stuff we have done overseas is now brought right back to our own front yards. America's chickens are coming home to roost."

To address the mounting concern about potential damage from his association with such an extremist nutcase, Barack did what Barack seems to most love doing: he gave a speech talking about −Barack!− and lecturing us to try to be as appreciative of him as possible.

Knowing how certain it was that his allies in the media would cover for him by proclaiming it a great speech and asserting that it had put the whole matter behind him, he stood in a setting that looked good and spun a message that sounded fine unless you actually thought about what he said, in which case his message was meaningless besides being deceptive.

Yes, Obama said, as he sat in that church he had heard Wright make remarks that *could be considered controversial.*

A crock! Makes it sound like he viewed Wright as some normal preacher speaking out against something understandably perceived as an injustice when, of course, the sort of views that Wright embraced and expressed were that America was far, far more bad than good, that racism is OK if you are black hating white, that the conflict in the Middle East is all the fault of the Jews and not at all related to radical Islam, etc.

Yes, Obama claimed, he strongly disagreed with many of Wright's political views, and, gosh, golly, doesn't that make him just like those of us who do not agree with everything our priest, minister of rabbi says?

A crock! There are very, very few priests, ministers and rabbis who preach the hatred for America that Jeremiah Wright preached – and any normal good American would not stand for it but instead stand up and walk out.

That's what Hillary Clinton said she would have done.

Apparently that's what Oprah Winfrey did. She had been a member of Wright's congregation but left. Why? You'd think the media would have hounded her asking why. But they didn't. How convenient for Barack. Suppose it had been George W. Bush or any conservative Republican who might have been embarrassed by the media's asking Oprah— think they would have still passed on doing so?

But Barack was permitted to get away with claiming that he had never heard Wright make any of these, or similarly outrageous, anti-American or racist statements, while he was in church at any time in 20 years of his attendance there without the media making any serious effort to point out the absurdity of his making such a claim.

OK, they could have pressed him – as they would have a George Bush or any conservative – you have seen the tapes, are you comfortable being a member of a congregation that not only tolerates his saying such things but actually stands up and shouts its approval of what he says? Would you have been one of the ones giving Wright a standing ovation? What would you have done?

Never asked of him. Wonder why?

Nor, or course, did they point out that Wright's outrages were routinely printed in the church's newsletter which the Obamas received and then ask if he had missed it all there, too.

Were it a George W. Bush or any conservative feigning not realizing that Wright had actually ever said such things, wouldn't the media come straight after him with some ridiculing questioning, such as: You are claiming that for

20 years you have sat in Wright's church and socialized with him outside church and yet you never had a clue that he says things this nuts, and you are asking the American people to make you the person in command of all the country's intelligence operations. Why should voters trust you with figuring out what is best for our national intelligence when in 20 years you say you could not figure out what Rev. Jeremiah Wright was saying in the very church that you regularly attend?

Thanks to the aggressive indifference of the news media, the Rev. Wright issue faded. They simply would not talk much about it.

And then one day late in the primary election campaign season up popped Jeremiah Wright at the National Press Club where during a question and answer session he appeared to suggest that Barack really deep down agreed with him, dismissing Barack's supposed distancing from him as fake, saying: "Politicians say what they say and do what they do because of electability."

Having said previously, during his great excuse speech the media touted so much, that, "I can no more disown him than I can disown the black community; I can no more disown him than I can my white grandmother...," Barack calculated that it was either disown Wright or kiss the election goodbye.

So...long after Oprah had, long after Hillary Clinton would have, long after almost anyone else but a Jeremiah Wright cultist would have, Barack bailed and quit Wright's church.

He declared: "The person I saw yesterday (Wright saying, in effect, that he and Barack were birds of a feather) is not the person that I met 20 years ago."

A crock!

The media could have asked: But isn't he the same guy he was weeks ago when you said you could never disown him, the same guy that you invited to sit down with you and Michelle to bless your campaign as you launched it?

The media could have asked: Isn't he the same guy you previously described this way: "(Rev. Wright) is a sounding board for me to make sure that I am speaking as truthfully about what I believe as possible and that I'm not losing myself in some of the hype and hoopla and stress that's involved in national politics"?

The media could have asked: Wasn't your "sounding board" telling you with his comments at the National Press Club that you are not "speaking as truthfully" about what you really believe and that what you really believe is really a lot more like what he really believes than you are letting on?

Yeah, they could have asked these sorts of questions. Should have. Didn't.

Barack's long and close association with Jeremiah Wright should have been a truly important issue in the 2008 campaign because it speaks to his judgment.

It still does, which means it still deserves to be a focus in any campaign in which he is involved.

So does his association with Bill Ayers.

Barack's association with the unrepentant domestic terrorist Ayers raises this question that the media could never, of course, be expected to phrase in exactly this manner, but John McCain should have:

What do Barack Obama and Osama bin Laden have in common?

Answer: They both associate with people who have bombed the Pentagon.

For the longest time the mainstream media turned a blind eye and deaf ear to questions being raised in conservative media about Obama's close ties to Bill Ayers and his wife, Bernardine Dohrn, another unrepentant domestic terrorist who was at one time on the FBI's "Most Wanted" list.

Finally, at an April 16, 2008, television debate between

Obama and Hillary Clinton, George Stephanopoulos of ABC News and various official Democratic Party posts mentioned the Ayers matter and asked Barack to "explain that relationship."

Amazingly, up until this late point no one else in the major media had asked Obama this.

Amazingly – but perhaps not surprisingly – some in the Obama-fawning media tried to make the issue not that Obama should be scrutinized for associating with the likes of a Bill Ayers but rather that Stephanopoulos should be pilloried for asking him to explain the association.

Stephanopoulos, they pointed out— correctly— had ties to the Clintons and should never have been permitted to appear as a "journalist" putting questions to these two candidates when he had worked in the Clinton White House.

Fair point. Yet those who raised it never acknowledge the unfairness run rampant in today's major media wherein Republican candidates are routinely subjected to having to deal with former Democratic Party flacks major media outlets now proclaim to be "journalists."

Also supposedly unfair on the part of Stephanopoulos was that during an interview with FOX News commentator Sean Hannity he had been asked by Hannity why the mainstream media was so steadfastly avoiding asking Obama about his association with Ayers.

So to some of these Obama boosters in the media the fact that someone who so clearly did not favor Obama had urged that he be asked a certain question should be reason enough to not ask it.

At any rate, Barack tried to explain it all away this way:

"This is a guy who lives in my neighborhood, who's a professor of English in Chicago, who I know and who I have not received some official endorsement from. He's not somebody who I exchange ideas from on a regular basis. And the notion that somebody who engaged in detestable acts 40 years ago when I was eight years old somehow reflects on me and my values doesn't make much sense."

Contrary to the disingenuous claim by the Obama-protecting New York *Times* that "the two men do not appear to have been close," what Barack tried to pass off here as an explanation was a complete crock.

Just a guy in the neighborhood? Hardly.

Just a professor of English? Hardly.

Not someone he exchanges ideas with on a *regular* basis? Does he? Has he? Absolutely.

And so what if an unrepentant terrorist you choose to pal around with is a lot older than you are?

Yes, Barack was just a kid when Ayers was building and placing bombs trying to kill Americans right here in the United States – but that proves nothing one way or the other when it comes to the matter of whether he and Ayers are birds of a feather ideologically.

Actually, Barack was working closely with Ayers at the time Ayers was quoted in the New York *Times* on the very day of the 9/11 attacks as saying about his acts of terrorism against US targets that not only would he "do it again" but expressed regret that "I didn't do enough" – and Barack's reaction to that was to keep right on associating with Ayers. Actually, Barack had not just worked *with* Ayers; he had, in fact, worked *for* Ayers.

For a period of years Obama worked for the Ayers-founded *Chicago Annenberg Challenge*. Working together, the two men directed more than $100 million dollars to groups working to instill in students a commitment to radical politics. As Ayers told Venezuelan dictator Hugo Chavez, "We share the belief that education is the motor-force of revolution."

Over the years, joined together in a common cause and

deciding together just who to bestow tens of millions of dollars upon, how likely is it that the two men did not exchange ideas on a regular basis?

Think Ayers would have trusted Obama with such a role in the disbursement of so much money if he did not have good reason to believe that Obama and he were birds of a feather ideologically?

And that was not the only place Obama worked closely with Ayers. The two also spent a lot of time working together with the *Woods Foundation*, another dispenser of money to left-wing groups including a particular favorite of Barack's, *ACORN*, best known for its efforts to facilitate voter fraud. Together Ayers and Obama directed *Woods Foundation* money to their *Chicago Annenberg Challenge* and to individuals and groups who helped raise money to advance Barack's political aspirations.

True enough, Barack had not received "some official endorsement" from Bill Ayers. Of course not! An official endorsement from the likes of Ayers in his campaign for president would be the kiss of death.

But his explanation about their relationship conveniently omitted the fact that Ayers had indeed officially endorsed him previously when he ran for public office, not only donating to his campaign, but, in fact, hosting at his home, along with his fellow unrepentant domestic terrorist wife, the event that launched Barack's political career.

(Aside: Ayers was not the only embarrassingly radical character to have hosted a fund-raiser for Barack. So, too, had former Yasser Arafat spokesperson Rashid Khalidi, who, coincidentally enough, was the beneficiary of $110,000 of *Woods Foundation* largess thanks to Barack and Ayers. The media found this to be of little interest.)

The major media never made a serious inquiry into the matter of what-did-Barack-known-about-Ayers-and-when-did-he-know-it.

Instead, they gave him a pass. They ran a protection racket for him for free.

Even as late as a few weeks before Election Day they continued to accept the sort of excuse he offered up in an October 8th radio interview in which he said, "I assumed that he had been rehabilitated."

Such an "assumption," an alert and unbiased media would have detected and reported, is a crock.

Barack assumed this even after Ayers' 9/11 quotes in the New York *Times* about his domestic terrorist days in which he said he'd do it all over again and only regretted not doing more of it?

Barack assumed this despite the fact that Bill Ayers and his wife Bernardine Dohrn made it crystal clear they did not consider themselves "rehabilitated" and were unabashedly unrepentant in articles about them that appeared while Barack was working alongside Ayers. It is highly unlikely Barack could have been unaware of them since such articles appeared in both major local newspapers—the Chicago *Tribune* and the Chicago *Sun-Times* – as well as in the New York *Times* and *USA Today*.

What are the odds that you don't notice or hear about it when "a guy in the neighborhood" with whom you have been closely associated for a good while appears on the front cover of a magazine stomping on the American flag? What are the odds you wouldn't read the accompanying article about why he would do such an outrageous thing?

People foolish enough to buy Barack's explanations minimizing his association with Ayers to just being neighborly would probably fall, as the new media mostly did, for this testimony to his veracity offered up by his campaign strategist David Axelrod:

"Bill Ayers lives in his neighborhood. Their kids attend the same school. They're certainly friendly; they know each other, as anyone whose kids go to school together."

At the time, Barack's kids were ages 9 and 6; Ayer's kids were in their late 20's and early 30's.

As likely they attended school together as it is that what Barack said in explaining his relationships with Wright and Ayers is anything but a total crock.

*Can he possibly be
as inept at foreign affairs
as he is with the economy?*

Yes, he can!
Yes, he can!

*"People of the world— look at Berlin,
where a wall came down, a continent
came together, and history proved that
there is no challenge too great for
a world that stands as one."*

৪৩

The Berlin Wall came down because the world stood as one?

What a crock!

Those remarks from a July 24, 2008, campaign speech delivered in Berlin, Germany, should have been— and still are – a warning that Barack is in deep over his head, a man woefully ignorant of history, muddle-minded, so naïve and shallow in his thinking as to sometimes, as evidenced here, have difficulty discerning hard cold fact from mere wishful thinking.

The world stood as one?

Not the world everyone else was living in.

In the real world, the United States of America and the West stood on one side against on the other side a ruthless, relentless, callous Soviet Communist enemy and that "Cold War" raged for more than four decades.

We won.

They lost.

And *then* the Berlin Wall came down.

It didn't happen because the world got together and stood as one.

It happened because great leaders like Ronald Reagan, Pope John Paul II and Margaret Thatcher got together, stood strong, and made it happen.

"The Cold War reached a conclusion because of the actions of many nations over many years, and because the people of Russia and Eastern Europe stood up and decided that its end would be peaceful."

෮

Heaven forbid that Barack give any credit to President Ronald Reagan.

Heaven forbid that he give any credit to the United States of America.

No, it just happened— it just happened to have "reached a conclusion" because of the actions of "many" nations.

None of which are worth mentioning.

Except Russia.

Its people and the people of Eastern Europe simply "stood up and decided" that the end of the Cold War would be peaceful.

Isn't that nice? What a shame it didn't occur to them to stand up and decide this sooner.

To think that for four decades just about everyone but Barack was under the impression that the people of Russia had no say in what went on in their own country let alone in others.

Just about everyone else but Barack was under the impression that people living under a dictatorship— such as was the fate of the people of Russia and Eastern Europe — were dictated to. That standing up and deciding what they really want is not what people living under totalitarian regimes do.

Some – but apparently not Barack – seem to recall that people in Eastern Europe got gunned down or imprisoned if they were to do something that might be construed as trying to stand up and decide.

Just ask Eastern Europeans, such as Hungarians who stood up to Soviet tanks in Budapest in the 1956 uprising bloodbath, or Russians who were shipped off to the Gulag.

The people who lived under Communism during the Cold War remember what Barack forgot or never learned. It's why they've erected so many monuments to President Ronald Reagan and Pope John Paul II.

"Given our interdependence, any world order that elevates one nation or group of people over another will inevitably fail."

જી

This statement Barack made in his much-touted speech in Cairo, Egypt, on June 4, 2009, is without a doubt the most asinine thing ever said about America's role in the world by a President of the United States.

The "world order" is doomed to failure if one nation is elevated above any other?

(The nation he leads is, of course, elevated above *all* others.)

He was telling his Muslim audience, and the rest of the world listening in, that it is a terrible thing that America outshines countries like theirs and what the world needs is for America to decline so they can rise.

Why would a President of the United States ever stand before a foreign audience and lament the fact that America is such an exceptional country and suggest that the world would be a better place were we not?

And just who or what does he think elevated us? He stated as if it were fact that there is some sort of "world order" that elevates countries. There isn't.

Didn't America elevate itself? And isn't that a good thing, rather than some bad thing that he thinks will cause the world to fail?

The thinking – or lack of thought – that he displayed here is shocking and alarming.

Doesn't Barack have any clue as to why America is so elevated in the world? Think freedom and our free market economic system have something to do with it? No "world order" made us number one.

And if he thinks it is really possible that all countries can have equal standing in the world– never one being elevated above another– shouldn't he explain why this has never occurred throughout all history and why and how he thinks it could? And shouldn't the media have asked him this?

"I suspect that the Brits believe in British exceptionalism and the Greeks believe in Greek exceptionalism."

&

Barack clearly thinks that Barack is exceptional and has no qualms about saying so – but when it comes to agreeing with most of his fellow Americans— and so many non-Americans as well -- that the United States of America is exceptional, it's, well, not so fast.

Not that we should expect the President of the United States to roam the world boasting that America is so much better than all others like he does about himself.

But isn't it an embarrassment to the country when Barack makes it his practice while out of the country to literally bow down before foreign leaders and go out of his way to try to find things to apologize for about his country?

He is uncomfortable defending the notion that America is an exceptional country.

Bad enough.

But why, especially when standing on foreign soil, does he insist on labeling America's dealings with the world as "arrogance" and "dismissive, even derisive."

Doesn't it appear that Barack's view is that foreigners will become fonder of us if he seems to suggest that *he* is really not all that fond of us?

"I know that there has been controversy about the promotion of democracy in recent years, and much of this controversy is connected to the war in Iraq. So let me make it clear: no system of government can or should be imposed upon one nation by any other."

৪৩

The promotion of democracy is so controversial? Says who? And, so what?

But only "recently"?

And it's because of the war in Iraq?

And this is why Barack has decided to "make it clear" that a system of government cannot and should not be imposed on a country?

Well...

Didn't we Americans impose upon Germany a system of government that enabled its citizens to have the freedom to choose their leaders?

Didn't we Americans impose upon Japan a system of government that enabled its citizens to have the freedom to choose their leaders?

Does Barack think we could not?

We did.

Does he think we should not have?

"I will rebuild our military to meet future conflicts. But I will also renew the tough, direct diplomacy that can prevent Iran from obtaining nuclear weapons and curb Russian aggression."

୬

No one in the audience could be heard laughing out loud when Barack said this during his speech accepting the Democratic Party nomination for president in 2008.

Everyone should be laughing now.

Laughing at what he said, that is.

But worrying about what he has done.

Having already sharply curtailed the Reagan-inspired national ballistic missile defense system, having already slapped allies such as Poland and the Czech Republic by backing off on deploying missile defense setups in East Central Europe to try to appease Russia's Vladimir Putin, on January 5, 2012, Barack announced that his plan to "rebuild" America's military is to cut back our military might so sharply that, his administration acknowledged, it would no longer be possible for the United States to be able to fight a two front war.

"The tide of war is receding," he said in announcing his plan to further decimate a US military that is already stretched thin and working with outdated equipment at a time when threats to the security of the United States are soaring, not receding.

As for preventing Iran from obtaining nuclear weapons by renewing tough diplomacy, what tough diplomacy?

When Iranian citizens by the thousands poured into the street of Tehran protesting the power grab by the great nutcase Mahmoud Ahmadinejad and Barack stood silent and went golfing, do you suppose Ahmadinejad was intimidated by that notion of "tough diplomacy"?

And is Iran closer or further away from obtaining nuclear weapons with Barack as president? Take a wild guess.

"Tonight we heard President Bush say that the surge in Iraq is working when we know that's just not true."

ೞ

Was President Geroge W. Bush lying when he said that the surge in Iraq was working?

That's what Barack charged on January 29, 2008, twelve days before announcing his candidacy for the presidency.

He was, it seemed, buying into the view that Democratic Senate Majority Leader Harry Reid had expressed nine months earlier: "This war is lost."

But only months after calling Bush a liar for saying that the surge was working, on September 5, 2008, under questioning from Bill O'Reilly of FOX News, Barack sheepishly acknowledged that: "The surge is succeeding in ways that nobody anticipated."

Nobody?

Maybe Barack never anticipated it, but...

What about our commanding general in Iraq, General David Petraeus, who created and implemented that surge strategy? Didn't he anticipate it would succeed?

When the left-wing group *MoveOn.org* ran a full-page ad in the New York *Times* accusing the general of treasonous conduct, claiming that he was "constantly at war with the facts," and calling him "General Betray Us," it disgusted the country so much that the US Senate by a vote of 72-25 passed a resolution condemning the ad. Barack ducked out on voting, although he had just moments before been available to vote on another measure.

What about Senator John McCain who thought Reid was wrong to see the war as lost and Petraeus right in thinking his surge strategy would work and did his best to convince President Bush to back it?

What about President George W. Bush? Didn't he, like Senator McCain and General Petraeus, anticipate what Barack had not been able to?

"All of us are deeply disturbed by the, err, crashing of, err, the English Embassy, err, the embassy of the United Kingdom."

છ૭

"It was also interesting to see that political interaction in Europe is not that different from the United States Senate. There's a lot of – I don't know what the term is in Austrian – wheeling and dealing."

"Could an Obama win restore America's global image?" read a headline ABC News posted on its website days before Election Day 2008.

Fawning over Obama no more so than all the rest of the so-called mainstream media were doing at the time, ABC News gushed: *One week before Election Day, the world is revising its opinion of America. After a drop of confidence in the United States, presidential candidate Barack Obama has revived the U.S. brand, exporting a vision of American renewal to a world watching the election with unprecedented interest.*

Barack was telling the country that he would "restore America's image in the world" but it never seemed to occur to him, or to his media allies, that if some foreigners had an unfavorable image of the United States of America it could mean something is wrong with their judgment as opposed to being certain proof that there is something wrong with us.

But the media message was: President George W. Bush is a moron who says and does really dopey things— but Barack is just so brilliant and knowledgeable and wonderful.

Do you suppose that if President Bush had taken his merry time to express disapproval about an Iranian mob ransacking an embassy of our close ally, tossing bombs around it, stealing its classified documents and burning its flag, the media would have called attention to his having to be asked?

Think they would have mocked him royally had he referred to it as the *English* embassy when there has never in history been an *English* embassy or a *UK* embassy— it's the *British* embassy.

Might they have mocked Bush if he had said he didn't know how to say something in Austrian, a language a US president should know does not exist?

"Compared to some of the giants of history who've received this prize— Schweitzer and King; Marshall and Mandela— my accomplishments are slight."

ଞ

"I do not bring with me today a definitive solution to the problems of war."

Compared to some of the giants of history previously selected, Barack's accomplishments were slight?

Some? Only *some?* How about *all?*

And to think some deem him narcissistic.

He was nominated for the Nobel Peace Prize, which includes a gold medal and 10 million Swedish kronor (US$1.4 million) just twelve days after being sworn in as president– 12 days! Asked why more than 200 other nominees had been cast aside in favor of Barack, Nobel Committee head Thorbjoern Jagland said: "It was because we would like to support what he is trying to achieve."

So...Barack's achievement was *trying.*

"Only very rarely has a person to the same extent as Obama captured the world's attention and given its people hope for a better future," the Norwegian committee said in a statement.

He was for hope. And he was trying. Good enough for one of the world's great honors.

Bestowing the prize on Barack for hoped-for accomplishment as opposed to any actual accomplishment was "a clear signal that we want to advocate the same as he has done," the committee of five Norwegians admitted. Translated that means: *we five didn't like George W. Bush, so there!*

Barack was not asked by the media to name any of the giants of history compared to whom his achievements might *not* be slight. Nor did he volunteer the names of any.

As for his not having brought with him a *definitive* solution to the problems of war," somehow the media forgot to inquire as to which *tentative* ones he might have brought with him.

"Nearly one year ago, on a clear November night, people from every corner of the world gathered in the city of Chicago or in front of their television sets to watch..."

❧

The Nobel Prize ceremony in Oslo, Norway, was neither the first nor the only time Barack has spouted embarrassingly narcissistic gibberish during his on-going quest to improve America's image abroad.

When the *International Olympic Committee* met in Copenhagen, Denmark, to decide which city should host the 2016 Summer Olympics and Paralympics, the four cities still under consideration were Madrid, Spain, Tokyo, Japan, Rio de Janeiro, Brazil and an American city—Chicago. Many felt Chicago had the edge.

So off to Copenhagen to seal the deal went Barack to make a personal presidential pitch for his city, taking along wife Michelle and their fellow Chicagoan pal, talk show queen Oprah Winfrey. They picked Rio instead.

"As much of a sacrifice as people say this is for me or Oprah or the president to come for these few days," the first lady began her remarks to one group, sparing them any grim details of the sacrifice involved in having to fly over aboard a luxury government 757 jet and then having to stay at a grand hotel and endure the burden of attending an *International Olympic Committee* wine-and-cheese party and a luncheon hosted by Denmark's Queen Margaret II.

Those people who were saying what a sacrifice it was for this woman who was proud of her country for the first time in her adult life only after Barack became a US Senator running for president and who had called America "just downright mean" were undoubtedly quite impressed that she was making this sacrifice for an American cause.

Barack opted not to re-draw attention to the sacrifices they had endured to be there and instead chose to talk about his favorite subject, reminding the IOC that Chicago was the city to which "people from all over the world" had come to see— *him.*

*"Few would have foreseen on that day
that a united Germany would be led
by a woman from Brandenburg
or that their American ally would
be led by a man of African descent."*

℘

Fred J. Eckert

On November 9, 2009, people from throughout the world gathered in Berlin, German, to commemorate the 20th anniversary of the fall of the Berlin Wall.

Among the world leaders in attendance: British Prime Minister Gordon Brown, French President Nicolas Sarkozy and, of course, German Chancellor Angela Merkel.

Even Russian President Dmitry Medvedev attended.

The no-show: The leader of the very country most responsible for the fall of the wall— the President of the United States.

When Barack was looking for a backdrop to use to feign foreign policy credentials before a fawning news media he picked Berlin because both Ronald Reagan and John F. Kennedy are fondly remembered for remarks they made there.

In 2008 the German magazine *Der Spiegel* summed up Barack's visit as "People of the World, Look at Me."

In 2009, Berlin having served its usefulness for Obama, an understandably angry about the snub *Der Spiegel* reported his absence as "Barack Too Busy."

Pleading a too busy schedule– not true– Barack instead sent a video of remarks he would have made had he bothered to attend.

In his taped remarks he mentioned the day President Kennedy had spoken at the Berlin Wall – but not the day that President Reagan had – and he made a point that had probably not occurred to anyone else and that probably no one else would have ever thought of mentioning.

Few would have known that day Kennedy spoke there that one day we would all have— *him.*

What did Barack say at the
state funeral in Poland?

ॐ

When throngs gathered in and near Wawel Cathedral in Krakow, Poland, on April 18, 2010, for the state funeral mass for Polish President Lech Kaczynski and his wife, Maria, this time Barack did not embarrass himself and his country by anything he said there.

Instead, he embarrassed himself and his country by what he did.

The Polish president and his wife were among those who had died in one of the most tragic airplane crashes of recent times, a crash that killed all 96 passengers aboard – 80% of the top echelon of the government of Poland as well as many of that country's foremost military and religious leaders.

The Polish government Tu-154 jet went down while trying to land in dense fog at Smolensk in western Russia. All aboard were on their way to attend a 70th anniversary memorial ceremony at the nearby site of the Katyn Forest Massacre, an historic event of enormous significance to Poles, where thousands of Polish military officers taken prisoner by the Soviet Communists when they invaded Poland in 1939 in support of Hitler's Nazi Germany had been brutally executed by the Soviet NKVD secret police acting on the direct orders of Joseph Stalin.

Leftists in denial about Communist brutality long claimed that either Katyn never happened or that it was the Nazis who did it, but in 1989 Soviet Premier Mikhail Gorbachev publicly admitted that on direct orders from Stalin some 25,700 Poles had been shot and buried at Katyn and two other sites.

Thus a current great tragedy for Poles that linked to the memory of another great tragedy for Poles made the mourning in Krakow so very special.

Barack, of course, made plans to attend. But something came up that caused him to cancel: He had put together a foursome, so instead he went golfing.

"Islam has demonstrated through words and deeds the possibilities of religious tolerance..."

Islam = religious tolerance.

Many of us are not as acutely aware of this as Barack is, but he says he has seen it demonstrated in words and in deeds.

Oh, the possibilities revealed unto him!

Presumably he felt that the Muslim audience listening to him in Cairo, and listening in from other lands, had no need for him to remind them of any specific examples he had in mind of words used by Islamists to foster religious tolerance or deeds Islamists have performed in their efforts to demonstrate the possibilities of religious tolerance.

What about these words of Iran's Ayatollah Khomeini: "Islam says, 'Kill all the unbelievers...Kill them, put them to the sword!'"?

These words of Osama bin Laden: "We do our duty of fighting for the sake of the religion of Allah"?

What about deeds such as the 9/11 "Death to Infidels" attack or the attacks against US embassies and US military personnel or all the attacks targeting Christian and Jewish civilians around the world?

When Salman Rushdie wrote a book critical of Islam and a Danish cartoonist drew something some Muslims did not like death warrants were issued.

In many Muslim countries renouncing Islam for another faith is a capital crime and there is an absolute ban on any religion other than Islam. In many Muslim countries it is common practice to terrorize Christians, and death and disfigurement await anyone who dares criticize the Qur'an.

From the media fawning that Barack received over his Cairo speech you'd think Lincoln was back with the Gettysburg Address.

They never asked him which words and deeds demonstrated Islamic religious tolerance? Never asked: Isn't it the Christian world, not Islam, where one finds religious tolerance?

"Islam carried the light of learning through so many centuries, paving the way for Europe's renaissance and enlightenment."

൮

"It was innovation in Muslim communities that developed the order of algebra, our magnetic compass and tools of navigation, our mastery of pens and printing, our understanding of how disease spreads and how it could be healed."

൮

"Islamic culture has given us majestic arches and soaring spires, timeless poetry and cherished music, elegant calligraphy, and places of peaceful contemplation."

It is laughable when Muslim supremacists make the ridiculous claim that Western Civilization owes it all to the Muslim world.

But when a President of the United States so thoughtlessly echoes it – and does not get called on it by the news media— it's time to worry about how far along the dumbing down is.

Instead of just focusing on where Barack was saying this— overseas— and the fact that the audience was large and consisted of Muslims, a media half as interested in truth as it is in frivolous fawning would have done some fact-checking and asked Barack to explain a few things. Such as:

What about all those Catholic monks in all those European monasteries who painstakingly copied manuscripts during the period between the fall of the Roman Empire and the Renaissance? Weren't they, not Muslims, really the ones who "carried the light of learning through many centuries" and deserve the credit for preserving Western Civilization?

Ever hear of the German Johannes Gutenberg and what he did for our mastery of printing?

Wasn't the magnetic compass invented in China during the days of the Qin dynasty?

Wasn't it the Europeans with their ship building and sailing tools of navigation skills who enabled the great voyages of oceanic discovery?

Ever heard that Archimedes of Sicily was the inventor of the arch? Heard of the Roman arch?

No timeless poetry and cherished music without Islam?

For mindless comment, to top the Muslim supremacist nonsense of his Cairo speech, Barack might have to go to Switzerland and heap praise upon the Swiss for inventing the hole and marvel about how they export them packed in cheese.

"Around the world the Jewish people were persecuted for centuries, and anti-Semitism in Europe culminated in an unprecedented Holocaust... On the other hand..."

৪৩

On the other hand?

The Obama cheerleaders in the media – and some other muddle-minded people as well— in their never ending striving for excuses to heap praise upon Barack seized upon his mentioning persecution of the Jews, anti-Semitism and the Holocaust before a Muslim audience in Cairo as some bold and courageous statement.

He does indeed deserve credit for saying some of what he said where he said it, specifically for his calling Holocaust denial "baseless, ignorant and hateful" and for stating that "threatening Israel with destruction or repeating vile stereotypes about Jews is deeply wrong."

However, his use of the phrase "but on the other hand" comes dangerously close to excusing his listeners from taking it all that seriously.

"But on the other hand, it is also undeniable that the Palestinian people— Muslims and Christians— have suffered in pursuit of a homeland. For more than sixty years they have endured the pain of dislocation..."

There is no moral equivalency and no excuse for giving any listener any grounds for thinking he is hearing it suggested that there might be.

Setting aside who is to be blamed for it— and it is Muslims every bit as much as non-Muslims— not getting land that you wish for is not the same as being gassed to death.

"I have unequivocally prohibited the use of torture by the United States, and I have ordered the prison at Guantanamo Bay closed by early next year."

બ

For any other President of the United States this would surely qualify as his biggest lie, dumbest statement and greatest insult to his own country.

With Barack, however, there's just too much to choose from to be so sure there's not another worse one out there somewhere.

Truth is, Barack has had nothing to do with prohibiting the use of torture.

Torture has always been illegal in the United States. He knows that.

What he was doing in saying this during his Cairo speech was deliberately pandering to— identifying with— an audience that put blind faith in charges made by radical Islamists, and others, that George W. Bush tortured prisoners, prisoners who were, of course, Islamic terrorists.

He was, in effect, saying that the Guantanamo Bay Detention Facility was a torture chamber and that is why, because of him, in just a few months it would be closing down.

Of course, as noted elsewhere, the Executive Order that he issued to close it was subsequently superseded by another Executive Order that he issued to keep it open after all.

It is one thing for foreigners who don't know better, and probably don't want to know better, to portray Americans as torturers, it is quite another for the President of the United States to not counter that and instead seem to nod in agreement.

While torture has always been illegal in the United States, it is almost a routine occurrence in many Muslim countries, not just condoned but encouraged by both church and state.

"As a student of history..."

ଓ

While some might rank Barack's making his "I am my brother's keeper" boast while doing nothing to assist his own brother who was living in deprivation as his greatest unintended laugh line, his boast in Cairo that he's "a student of history" is perhaps an equally great unintended laugh line.

It was promptly after bestowing this title upon himself that he proceeded to rattle off a litany of errors about history by attributing to the Islamic world, as noted earlier, inventions and other advancements for which history credits others.

He also, again as noted earlier, will be remembered as the president who during an address before a joint session of Congress got it wrong when elucidating upon the history of a great American president.

"Islam has always been a part of America's history" is another thing Barack said, while speaking in Cairo, that he apparently thinks proves him to be such a student of history.

Commenting on the mostly meaningless gibberish, absurd claims and historic errors of Barack's Cairo speech, *Newsweek* editor Evan Thomas babbled: "Obama's standing above the country, above – above the world, he's sort of God...He's the teacher. He is going to say, 'now, children, stop fighting and quarreling with each other.' And he has a kind of a moral authority that he – he can – he can do that."

The TV host to whom Evans said that, another one of those Democratic Party flacks masquerading as a "journalist," had once while anchoring news reporting about Barack's campaigning gushed, "I feel this thrill going up my leg."

Many students of history shudder at the very thought of such a president and such a news media.

Fool us twice?

"Fool me once, shame on you;
Fool me twice, shame on me."

Chinese proverb

ଉ

"The real question is, 'Will our country be better off four years from now? How will we lift our economy and restore America's place in the world?"

Barack Hussein Obama
4 years ago

৪১

Is America better off for having elected Barack Obama president?

Or did the country make a dreadful mistake by falling for a total crock?

Ronald Reagan famously asked the American people to ask themselves if they were better off than they were before having elected Jimmy Carter president— and come Election Day the people resoundingly answered that enough was enough, it was time to correct the terrible mistake and get the country back on track.

When George Stephanopoulos of ABC News and various official Democratic Party posts asked Barack during an October 3, 2011, interview if he thought the American people were better off than they were before he took office, he answered: "Well I don't think they are better off than they were four years ago."

No one else seems to either.

Indeed, it would be next to impossible to find anyone in his right mind who would claim that we are better off.

Now when Barack himself – a man who did not hesitate to make the claim that he can cause the oceans to stop rising and the planet to start healing— is afraid to risk being laughed at by claiming America is better off than we were four years ago, you know things are really, really bad.

The best he could come up with: "I think we are better off now than we would have been if I hadn't taken all the steps that we took."

Things could be even worse!

That's the best justification Barack can think of as a case for re-electing him president.Things are just awful, that's for sure – but, you know, there's always the possibility they could be even worse– what a campaign slogan to run on, huh?

Four years ago Barack managed to get elected president, not because of any record of achievement to point to as an indicator of great potential – there was none – but because his campaign and its cheerleaders in the news media were such remarkably effective con artists in selling a bill of goods that a record of accomplishments was unimportant and what really mattered was that he said things like "hope" and "change" and "Yes we can!, Yes, we can!" and "We are the ones we've been waiting for."

Didn't matter that it was all just a crock, the con worked.

But after the prose and the promises came the performance in office— and right now more and more Americans are finding it increasingly difficult to imagine how we could have made a worse choice for president.

This time, look for Barack and his allies in the media to do all they can to deflect focus from the true issue of 2012 – does his performance in office merit re-election or does it not?

Expect Barack and the Left to resort to a vicious smear campaign to destroy his opponent – and expect his media allies to assist him and cover for him just as they did last campaign and throughout his time in office.

As the campaign messages fill the airwaves you might want to think about a favorite of mine.

A Democratic governor of New York— whom I knew and often clashed with but respected and liked – used this campaign slogan in the primary election campaign in which he won his party's nomination:

"Before they tell you what they're going to do, make them show you what they've done."

Just as my friend Ronald Reagan suggested a great question to ask yourself before voting to re-elect a president, my friend Hugh Carey suggested a great test to demand of anyone asking for your vote for any high public office.

I suggest to you that the last thing that the Barack campaign and its media cheerleaders want you to do is to actually focus on what he has done and what he has failed to do.

Do that.

Also by Fred J. Eckert

Hank Harrison for President
Vandamere Press: ISBN 0-918339-24-3
- *"One of the best political spoofs since* The Mouse That Roared*" – Library Journal*
- *"Hillarious!" – Fort Worth Star-Telegram.*
- *"Great political satire" – Senator Bob Dole*
- *"It's funny!" – Governor Mario Cuomo*

FIJI: Pacific Paradise
Bison Books: ISBN 0-86124-295-5

FIJI: Some Enchanted Islands
Bison Group: ISBN 0-86124-916-X

TONGA: The Friendly Islands
Burgess Books: ISBN 978-0-9850055-9-7
Forward by then Crown Prince Tupouto'a,
King of Tonga George (Siaosi) Tupou V

Remember when America had a real president?

Featured on ABC News on the centennial of Ronald Reagan's birth, and showcased in the Washington *Times, Human Events* magazine and a number of other conservative publications, *Reagan On Rushmore* promotes the idea of adding President Ronald Reagan to Mount Rushmore by showing the concept in homes and offices across America.

This inspirational art work features one of Ambassador Eckert's images of Mount Rushmore from his award-winning *Images of Our World* collection onto which acclaimed aviation artist Ted Williams has incorporated Reagan into the granite mountain next to Lincoln. The late Jack Kemp called it: "Beautifully done, an inspirational work of the highest quality in every aspect— a truly fitting tribute."

This collector's item for Reagan admirers can be purchased at Amazon in three sizes as a digitally double-matted print. Or it can be ordered in six sizes as a gallery-wrapped Giclee canvas print online at www.AmbassadorEckertImages.com or at Amazon.

Acknowledgements

I probably would not have gone ahead with this project had I not first been assured that my good friend Ted Williams would find the time to create the cover and advise and assist in the design and give me his feedback on the writing as well.

Ted created the cover for my political satire novel, *Hank Harrison for President*. The *Reagan On Rushmore* art image blends one of my photographic images and Ted's imaging onto it of Ronald Reagan. I am a huge fan of his art. Check it out at www.tedwilliamsillustration.com

Other good friends who were kind enough to review my work and give me the benefit of their comments and suggestions are: Tom Gosdeck, Mary Grabar, Susan Lewis, Rich Stowe and Russ Surber.

As always, I am indebted to my three children— Doug, Brian and Cindy— for their encouragement and for their comments and suggestions.

Most of all, I am indebted to my wife, Karen, who is always my best editor and always my biggest source of encouragement.

About the author

Fred J. Eckert has been a US Ambassador, a Member of Congress, a state senator, the elected chief executive of a large municipal government, a novelist, an author, an advertising and public relations executive, a small businessman and ranks as a professional photographer.

President Ronald Reagan called him "a good friend and valuable advisor...a man of great experience and wisdom."

His exemplary performance in public office was the subject of an admiring *Reader's Digest* profile and also drew accolades for his statesman stance from many other leading publications, including The New York *Times, The Wall Street Journal* and every other major newspaper in New York State.

His writing has appeared in such national magazines as *Outdoor Life, The Wall Street Journal* and *Reader's Digest*; in a number of conservative on-line publications, including *Human Events, American Thinker, Pajamas Media, National Review Online* and The Washington *Examiner*; and in nearly every major newspaper in the United States.

His political satire novel, *Hank Harrison for President,* was acclaimed by *Library Journal* as "one of the best political spoofs since *The Mouse That Roared.*" He is author-photographer of three photo books— two on Fiji and one on Tonga.

He has lectured on the South Pacific at *The Smithsonian Institution* and debated international terrorism at England's *Oxford University Union*, the world's oldest and most prestigious debating society.

He lives with his wife, Karen, in Raleigh, North Carolina. They have three grown children and four grandchildren.

CPSIA information can be obtained at www.ICGtesting.com
Printed in the USA
LVOW131123230912

299924LV00002B/112/P